The Old Nubian Language

Dotawo ▸
Monographs

3

Dotawo ▸ Monographs

Series Editors Giovanni Ruffini
Vincent W.J. van Gerven Oei

Design Vincent W.J. van Gerven Oei
Typeset in 10/12 Skolar PE, Lucida Sans Unicode, and Antinoou.

Cover image Throne Hall, Old Dongola.
Photo by Vincent W.J. van Gerven Oei, 2016.

Dotawo ▸ is an imprint of punctum books, co-hosted by DigitalCommons@Fairfield

THE OLD NUBIAN LANGUAGE. Copyright © 2017 Eugenia B. Smagina and José Andrés Alonso de la Fuente. This work carries a Creative Commons BY-NC-SA 4.0 International license, which means that you are free to copy and redistribute the material in any medium or format, and you may also remix, transform, and build upon the material, as long as you clearly attribute the work to the authors (but not in a way that suggests the authors or punctum books endorses you and your work), you do not use this work for commercial gain in any form whatsoever, and that for any remixing and transformation, you distribute your rebuild under the same license.

http://creativecommons.org/licenses/by-nc-sa/4.0/

Originally published as Е.Б. Смагина, *Древненубийский язык.* – Ю.Н. Завадовский & Е.Б. Смагина, *Нубийский язык.* Москва, 1986.

First published in 2017 by punctum books, Earth, Milky Way.
https://punctumbooks.com/

ISBN-13: 978-1-947447-18-9 (print); 978-1-947447-19-6 (ePDF)
LCCN: 2017952350

Eugenia B. Smagina
The Old Nubian Language

Translated by José Andrés Alonso de la Fuente

Contents

Preface · ix

Translator's Foreword · · · · · · · · · · · · · · · 11

Introduction · · · · · · · · · · · · · · · · · · · 15

GRAMMAR

Script: Reconstruction of the Phonological System · · · · · · 23

Lexicon · 29

Morphology · 33

Syntax · 49

TEXT

The Miracle of Saint Menas · · · · · · · · · · · · · 59

References · 75

Preface

It is with great pleasure that we hereby present the English translation of Eugenia B. Smagina's *Древненубийский язык* (*The Old Nubian Language*) by Slavicist José Andrés Alonso de la Fuente.

Even though published in 1986, sixteen years before Gerald M. Browne's *Old Nubian Grammar*, this work is of great relevance to the history and field of Old Nubian studies. Not only does it show us that significant progress was made in understanding the language outside Western research institutions, on whose sole authority we all too often rely, it also expounds the subject with rigor and clarity.

In spite of the fact that since the publication of *Древненубийский язык* many new Old Nubian sources have been unearthed and considerable progress has been made in terms of understanding the language, Smagina's work will prove indispensable as a first encounter with this Nilo-Saharan language from the Medieval period, owing to the conciseness of its exposition.

Together with the work of Fritz Hintze and Gerald M. Browne, it should be considered indispensible to any investigation of Old Nubian grammar, and as such we are grateful to its translator for making this work finally available to those of us with poor knowledge of its original language.

Vincent W.J. van Gerven Oei
Giovanni Ruffini

Translator's Foreword

The present work is the English translation of the Old Nubian grammar by Eugenia B. Smagina (Russian: Евгéния Б. Смáгина) originally published in Russian in 1986. Some authors have noted on several occasions the appropriateness of having such a tool at the disposal of the global community of specialists in Nubian philology and linguistics, especially taking into account the marginal place Russian occupies as a language of scientific diffusion, at least in this field. Among those expressing that desideratum, the most notable is doubtlessly the *dôyen* of Nubian studies, the late Gerald M. Browne (1943-2004), who once, describing Smagina's Old Nubian grammar, affirmed that "this lucid, well-argued presentation should be available to all Nubiologists and ought therefore to be translated into a western language" (1991: 289).

Some remarks about the translation are in order. The list of abbreviations is provided below. In those few places where Smagina made a direct, contrastive comparison between ON and Russian, I have tried to adapt it so that English speakers may comprehend Smagina's point, and the comparison be still of some use.

As for contents, I dispensed with the data regarding contemporary Nubian languages in the prologue, especially a large fragment on p. 11 of the original. Bibliograpical references have been reduced to those concerning Old Nubian, and adapted to current conventions (I have also replaced Smagina 1977 by Smagina 1985, since the latter is far more easily accessible than the former). Many new works have appeared in the meanwhile. We recommend the reader to consult Jakobi & Kümmerle (1993) and the bibliography on the "Medieval Nubia" website.[1]

Generally speaking, while many of Smagina's interpretations are open to discussion, such a contrastive study with other ON grammars should be undertaken somewhere else. However, in order to ease the task, I provide the interested reader with an Appendix containing direct references to the corresponding sections in both

1   http://www.medievalnubia.info/dev/index.php/Guide_to_the_Texts

Smagina's grammar and two grammatical studies by Browne. If I have chosen Browne's over more classical treatments such as those by Zyhlarz or Hintze, it is because Browne's works are far more accessible and, in addition, Browne heavily relied and acknowledged the merits of his predecessors.

Since those works are organized in very distinct ways, this should allow a direct comparison without much consuming of time. With this goal in mind, I have introduced a numeration for each section – as everything which does not belong to the original text, they are in square brackets – so that cross-referencing with Browne's work should be more efficient.

The work on this translation has been made possible through the Juan de la Cierva postdoctoral Fellowship from Spain's Ministerio de Ciencia e Innovación (Ref. IJCI-2014-19343), for which I am very thankful. Likewise, I wish to express my deepest appreciation to my colleagues from the Departament de Ciències de l'Antiguitat i de l'Edat Mitjana (Universitat Autònoma de Barcelona) for providing the best conditions to complete the work (*moltes gràcies!*). Last but not least, I convey my sincerest gratitude to Angelika Jakobi and Vincet W.J. van Gerven Oei for having shared their expertise in the emergent field of Old Nubian philology, and to Giovanni Ruffini for having polished the text.

List of Abbreviations

Smagina used a handful of abbreviations for some of the examples in the body of the text.

1, 2, 3	person
ABS	absolutive
ACC	accusative
GEN	genitive
NOM	nominative
PL	plural
SG	singular

Introduction

1   The Nubian language spreads across Eastern Africa, in the territory of two countries, Sudan and the Republic of Egypt, in the Valley of the Nile and in the mountains of the regions of Kordofan and Darfur, west of the White Nile river.

According to data from 1971, as shown in the *United Nations Demographic Yearbook*, one million of Nubians lives in Sudan, whereas around three hundred thousand live in Egypt.[1] Of the Nubians living in Sudan, around six hundred thousand are the so-called Hill Nubians and less than three hundred thousand are Nile Nubians.

Nubian is not a homogenous language, it breaks up into local dialects. Nubian dialects are divided into two groups: Nile Nubian and Hill Nubian.

There are three Nile Nubian dialects (four if we add the one spoken in Fadicca), and around eight Hill Nubian dialects:

1. Kenuzi, or Kunuzu, spoken in Egypt, up to the settlement of Korosko.
2. Mahass, spoken in Egypt and Sudan, from Korosko to the third cataract of the Nile.
3. Fadicca, a subdialect of Mahass. It is spread from Korosko to the settlement of Sukkot. There are no great differences between Fadicca and Mahas. Reinisch [54] considered Fadicca as an independent dialect, but sometimes mentioned the subdialectal distinction. Fadicca is the main descendent of the Old Nubian language.
4. Dongola, spoken in Sudan, from the third cataract of the Nile to the settlement of Korti.
5. Hill Nubian dialects, those spoken by the so-called Hill Nubians living in Sudan, west of the White Nile, on the Kordofan plateau (Kordofan dialects: Dair, Dilling, Ghulfan, Karko, Kadaru, Kundukur) and to the West of Kordofan, on the still more elevated plateau of Darfur (Darfur dialects: Midob, Birked).

---

1   These numbers in no way reflect the real linguistic situation: though Nubas are usually bilingual, many of them have forgotten their language altogether and speak only Arabic.

2   All the Nubians lived in the regions described above, until the building of the Aswan (High) Dam. As a result of the erection of the dam, the Nile Valley was submerged covering an extension of around 500 km, from the first cataract of the Nile to the settlement of Kosha (between the second and third cataract). In current times, those Nubians whose villages ended under water were removed to another location. This mainly affected to the speakers of Kenuzi and, partially, of Mahass. The rest of the Nubians lives where they always did until today.

The Nubians from Sudan were removed from submerged territories and relocated east of the Nile River in the basin of the Atbara River. There, close to the settlement of Khashm el-Girba, lands were assigned to that effect and the town of (New) Wadi Halfa was declared administrative center of the Nubians. The villages removed and reconstructed in this new location were named after their original designations and adding "New" in front [16].

The Nubians from Egypt back in time dwelt on what is now water-reservoir territory. They also were removed to the non-submerged area of upper Aswan, along the water-reservoir coasts in the region of Kom Ombo.

3   Unlike most non-Semitic languages of Afrika, Nubian can be divided into two different chronological layers: modern and medieval. The Nubian language found in monumental inscriptions is called Old Nubian (Russian древненубийский, German *Altnubisch*). Such a name shall be preserved in the present work.

In medieval times (from the 4th to the 14th century), the Nubians had three different kingdoms in the Nile Valley: Nobatia, Makuria (Muḳurra), and Alodia (Aloa, 'Alwa). At the beginning these kingdoms were free, but, at a latter stage, they succumbed to the Arabs. Old Nubian (henceforth, ON), the language of the medieval Nubians, survives until today in the manuscripts and inscriptions that were unearthen in Nobatian territory (between the first and the third cataract of the Nile). Missionaries from Byzantium came to Nubia in the middle of the sixth century. As told in Syrian and other medieval sources, those missionaries began to Christianize all the inhabitants of the three Nubian kingdoms [7]. The design of the Nubian script seems to be the result of their missionary activities, facilitating the spread of Christian literature among the Nubians with translations of Greek religious texts – and most likely Coptic too – into Old Nubian.

The earliest Nubian inscription with a datation, that is, the one found in Es-Sabu (Wadi es-Sebua), goes back to 795. The latest dated text is the manuscript of the Niceas canons (1035). Therefore, it is possible to affirm that the Old Nubian script was actively used for at least three centuries. Notwithstanding this, specialists take into consideration many other texts from earlier or latter periods.

In spite of Islam's fast spread during the medieval epoch in Egypt and Sudan, the Nubians kept being faithful to Christianism which only was only replaced by Islam several centuries later, when the Arabs invaded Egypt (Nobatia and Makuria in the 14th century, Alodia in the 16th century). The Islamization process took gradually place. It seems that it begun right away after the Arabian invasion of Egypt.

4   Old Nubian inscriptions were discovered by archaeologists only during the 19th century. But the bulk of ON texts which, as turned out, were enough to decipher the script was found at the beginning of the last century (in 1906). We know several long texts:

1. The account of one of the miracle of Saint Menas, of course, a translation of one of the chapters of the Greek hagiography (the original is not preserved). It is dated 985.
2. The homilly from the Pseudo-Nicene Canons. It is dated 1053.
3. The lectionary for the last days of the month of Khoiak (from the end of November to the end of December), preserved translation from Greek of fragments from the Evangelium of the Last Apostols.
4. The apocryphal legend of the apparition of Jesus to the Apostles in the Eleon mountain (the Mount of Olives), including the enumeration of 46 epithets for Christ.
5. A commercial agreement with 12 signatures. This is the most unintelligible of all texts.
6. The narration of the Nubian suffering of Christ of the so-called Pseudo-Chrysostom. This manuscript was found during the 1963-1964 excavation campaign in East Serre (Sudan). G.M. Browne has prepared a critical edition.
7. Few excerpts from the New Testament (there are only two fragments from the Old Testament, excerpts from the Psalms), edited by D. Barns [2], D.M. Plumley [14], and most of them by G.M. Browne [3-7]. These were found during excavation campaigns at the site of Qasr Ibrim (Primis in the medieval epoch) and other places in Nubia. Many more texts (around 85) were found in 1978, again in excavations in Qasr Ibrim.

Texts 1–5 were published by F. Griffith [28], the first two texts and the Legend of the Cross (text 4) in the monograph by Zyhlarz

[62]. The facsimile of one of those texts appeared in the work of Budge [9].

In addition, we know of many other manuscripts, graffiti, and ostraca preserved in fragmentary form. In this grammar, little mention will be made to those fragmentary materials and inscriptions. All instances will be taken from the best-preserved texts.

One part of these important ON texts may be found in the library of Berlin, another part in the British museum. Many Nubian inscriptions as well as fragments of manuscripts rest in the National Museum of Warsaw. The former ones were found by a team of Polish archeologists during the expedition to Faras and in other places [50].

The manuscript of the Pseudo-Chrysostom rests in the National Museum of Sudan (in Khartoum), where other ON texts may also be found.

5   The first decipherment of an ON inscription is due to H. Schäfer who co-authored along C. Schmidt two articles, published in 1906-1907, that contained all the texts known by the time [16, 17]. Thanks to the presence of Greek personal names and borrowings embedded in one of the texts (the Lectionary), as well as the supposition that words from modern Nubian dialects might be identified in some sections of the same text, these researchers were able to establish that one of the inscriptions appears to be a Greek translation of a passage from the New Testament. In sum, the Lectionary provided the key to understand the rest of texts.

In 1913 the monograph of F.Ll. Griffith sees the light of day. There, the author included all the texts known by the time, accompanied by the corresponding English translation, a short grammatical description of ON and a glossary [28]. To him belongs the credit of the decipherment of the ON script as well as the pioneering investigation on ON language structures.

The most important work on ON grammar is a monographic study by A. Zyhlarz [63], which includes a grammar, the text of three manuscripts and one inscription, the translation of these texts, and a glossary. Regrettably, Zyhlarz's grammar contains a good deal of half-worked statements, many of which do not stand up to serious scrutiny.

The well-known piece by the Dutch scholar B. Stricker [57] and the series of papers by the noted German Egyptologist F. Hintze [33], where various questions regarding ON phonetics (by Stricker) and morphology (by Hintze) are scrutinized, will follow.

Special mention deserve the most recent contributions by G.M. Browne, since they have the greatest impact on ON language research [21-23], especially those works devoted to morphology.

The first Russian work on ON texts is a paper by B.A. Turaev published in the journal *Христианский Восток* (The Christian Orient) in 1914. In that work, B.A. Turaev introduces the history of the finding and decipherment of ON texts to Russian philologists and provides the basics of their contents [13]. One of D.A. Ol'derogge's contributions [5] is devoted to the lexicon shared by Egyptian and Nubian. E.B. Smagina [8-12] elaborates on different issues regarding ON grammar.

6 As for the genealogical position of the Nubian language, there is no unanimous opinion. Some authors consider that Nubian occupies an isolated position among African languages, for it does not seem to belong to any known framily. There is a second opinion: A. Tucker considers that Nubian is a Nilotic language [58]. In his classification of the African languages, J. Greenberg included Nubian within the West-Sudanese branch of the Šari-Nile group of the Nilo-Saharan language family [27]. The issue about the genealogical classification of the Nubian languages, for the time being, remains unsolved. Recently, some authors have expressed the opinion that Nubian and Meroitic may have belonged to the Afro-Asiatic family in a branch by themselves (A.Ju. Militarev).

7 Examples and the sample text are given according to the most generally accepted transcription. Thus, an intervocalic dot stands for epenthesis which is supposedly realized as a laryngeal segment (see §18). [By "intervocalic dot" (= Browne's "raised point"), Smagina refers to the dot taken from the Bohairic revised orthography that appears over some vowels, see Stricker [57], where it is phonetically identified with the Arabic hamza.] A dot over "e" stands for a closed "e" (it may also be so that "e" with a point stands for "i").

Instances from three ON texts are given according to the numeration by Zyhlarz's in his monograph [63]. Text titles are abbreviated as follows: M – the Miracle of Mena; C – the homily from the Nicene Canons; Jn. – the Gospel according to John; Mth. – the Gospel according to Mathew; Mk. – the Gospel according to Mark, Gal. – Epistle of Paul to the Galatas, I and II Cor. – First and Second Epistle to Corinthians, Rom. – Epistle to Romans, Phil. – to Philippians, Heb. – Epistle to the Hebrews, St. – the Legend of the Cross ("St." stands for "the *Stauros*-text" and comes from Greek *staurós* 'cross,' which was borrowed into ON); PC – Pseudo-Chrysostom (page and line numbers are indicated); fragments from the Lectionary (L), and separately published fragments of biblical texts cited according to the generally accepted abbreviations; PS – Psalterium, Apoc. – Apocalypsis, chapter and verse numbers are indicated.

There is only one deviation from general convention: the transcription and transliteration of nasal sounds (see the table showing the ON consonants).

The author would like to express her gratitude to Gerald M. Browne (University of Urbana, Illinois) for having made accessible text editions and papers on the ON language which proved invaluable to writing the present work.

GRAMMAR

Script: Reconstruction of the Phonological System

8 The ON alphabet consists of 28 signs representing consonant as well as vowel phonemes.

It has also two diacritical marks (superscript): the line < ¯ > and the dot <˙>. The line is transliterated as *ı̄*, whereas the point is transliterated as such.

As follows from the table below, the ON alphabet is based on the Greek-Coptic model. This allows us to suppose that the first translators of biblical texts into ON were Copts or Greeks knowing Coptic. A total of 23 signs are of Greek origin, and three signs (*š, h, j*) as well as the diacritical marks are Coptic. Three signs (*ŋ, ñ, w*) have been taken, in all likelihood, from the Meroitic script, for they are not attested in Coptic.

Signs in parenthesis are used only in loanwords.

9 The analysis of ON texts and data from modern Nubian dialects allows us to say that each ON consonant sign represents a phoneme, while each vowel sign may represent various phonemes. Additionally, the diachronic analysis of ON texts allows us to speak not about phonetic features, but rather about the reconstruction of phonological oppositions. For example, the feature "frontal" is distinctive in the plosives of various modern Nubian dialects, and in some varieties the degree of aperture of some vowels depends on the presence of tones. Thus, the reconstruction of the ON phonological system can be done only in approximative terms.

10 In some modern Nubian dialects vowels are distinguished by quality, while in some others, by tones. But in ON such distinctive features have in most cases no graphic representation. Indeed, in order to mark /o/ they used two signs, i.e., <o> and <ω>. Although they appear to be allographs of one grapheme, sometimes their use fluctuate. In ON texts vowel length is marked by doubling the letter:

taa 'girl,' ŋoog 'house' (This doubling, however, could mean a laryngeal after the vowel). If we compare words such as šaa 'door' and ša 'spear,' ŋook 'fame' and ŋok- 'to go, pass (through),' we can conclude that vowel length was a distinctive feature already in ON. Put another way, every vowel sign had at least two different phonemic correlates.

Table 1. Old Nubian alphabet.

ⲁ	a	ⲓ	i, y	ⲥ	s	⳱	(h)
ⲃ	(b)	ⲕ	k	ⲧ	t	ϭ	j
ⲅ	g	ⲗ	l	ⲩ	i, w	ⲣ̄	ŋ
ⲇ	d	ⲙ	m	ⲫ	(ph)	ⳝ	ñ
ⲉ	e	ⲛ	n	ⲭ	(kh)	ⳟ	w
ⲍ	(z, ks)	ⲟ	o	ⲯ	(ps)	ⲟⲩ	u
ⲏ	ē?, i?	ⲡ	p	ⲱ	o	ⲉⲓ	i, y
ⲑ	(th)	ⲣ	r	ⳉ	š		

In ON there is no graphic distinction for the vowel feature of tone. However, if we compare, on one hand, ON homographs such as *ay* 'I' and *ay* 'heart, soul,' and, on the other, their counterparts in the Mahass language, it turns out that in Mahass those words are distinguished only by tone. Thus, it is possible that the homography of the previously mentioned pair of words (and of many others, being plentiful in ON texts, both lexical and morphological, e.g., *in* 'this' and *in-* 'to be' or the locative-ablative suffix *-lo* and the focal particle *-lo*) is not due to homonymy, but to the presence of distinctive tones.

11 Vowel /i/ is represented in different ways: with the help of one grapheme (there are three different letters to represent /i/, see Table 1), with a digraph, with a diacritical mark or with a combination of letter plus diacritical mark. The various representations of this vowel can occur in one and the same word. Moreover, context and the moment of the writing seem irrelevant: variants may appear in the very same manuscript. The diachronic analysis does not offer any telling conclusion. Thus, based on the fluctuating representation in the script, it is impossible to describe the distinctive features of /i/, such as tone or degree of aperture. The systematic description of all the graphic variants mentioned above and their functional load remains a task for the future.

12 The distinction in the script of the voiced and voiceless plosives requires some comment.

The use of letters representing voiced and voiceless plosives frequently fluctuates:

- t/d: *tappide/dappide* 'death'
- k/g: *ak-/ag-* 'to sit'
- p/(b): *-appa/-abba* 'because, since.' (The letter representing /b/ is found only in this word and in loanwords. On the other hand, modern dialects have not preserved the original /p/, for it has yielded /b/ or /f/: Dongolese *sarbe* 'finger' vs. ON *sarpe*, Dongolese *fogor* 'lame' – ON *pokod*.)

In ON the fricatives /s/ and /š/ do not have voiced correlates, and there is no voiceless counterpart for the affricate /j/.

Here the presence/absence of the feature "voice" is clearly ignored.

In the Greek inscriptions found on Nubian territory and redacted by Nubians, the most widespread orthographic mistake consists in the incapacity to distinguish between voiced and voiceless plosives: *toulos* instead of *doûlos* 'slave,' *gegeymenon* instead of *kekéymenon* 'recumbent (ACC),' *dyflon* instead of *typhlón* 'blind (ACC),' etc. This phenomenon can be sometimes observed in both Greek loanwords and proper names: Greek *eikṓn* 'image; icon' vs. ON *igon* (M, 43), Greek *Zacharías* 'Zachariah' vs. ON *sagarias* (trade agreement, see [29]).

The historical lenition of the ON plosives in certain positions is also attested.

Based on all these facts, it is possible to conclude that in ON the distinction voiced/voiceless was not expressed or was irrelevant. Maybe it played the role of influence of the Coptic language and graphic, where the distinction voiced/voiceless for most plosives is not phonemic.

13 If two vowel signs are written together, there will be most of times a dot over the second one: *uȯá* 'second,' *koȧŋa* (from 'to have'). This is how they adapted loanwords in case they have hiatus, e.g., Greek *archiereús* 'high priest' is graphically represented as *árkhiėreósi*. This means that hiatus was forbidden in ON, and when it appears on the morpheme boundary, they avoided it by inserting a kind of sound which is represented by the intervocalic dot. In two instances the hiatus is avoided by inserting a letter from the Coptic texts (sometimes present also in ON texts), i.e., the spirant /h/ (see Table 1). It is also possible that the intervocalic dot represents a laryngeal segment /h/.

14 In several examples from the vulgar register the liquid as well as the nasal /n/ are assimilated to the adjoining consonants (including other liquids). The assimilation is always total and, in the majority of cases, regressive.

Regressive assimilation

15 (1) The liquid /l/ is totally assimilated to the dental plosive /d/ and to both velar plosives, as well as to the nasal /n/ and /m/: *kulid-do* 'on the mountain' (*kul*, 'mountain,' *-i-l*, definite article, *-do*, superessive suffix); *ŋa-k-ka* 'son,' *ŋa-n-ni* 'son's' (*ŋa-l*, 'son,' *-ka*, accusative suffix, *-n(i)*, genitive suffix); *dum-men-es-s-in* 'should not, not fitting' (*dul-*, 'to be,' *-men-*, suffix of negation).

(2) The vibrant /r/ is totally assimilated to the sibilant /s/, the affricate /j/ (in the latter case, not always), to the nasal /n/ and to all the plosives (with the exception of /g/); to the latter the vibrant partially assimilates according to the place of articulation, e.g., *tit-ti* 'favour, grace' (*tir-*, 'to give,' *-ti*, nominal suffix); *tad-dal* 'with him' (*tar*, 3rd personal pronoun, *-dal*, comitative suffix); *tijj* 'to give (something)' (*tir-* 'to give,' *-j*, transitive suffix); *tekka* 'him' (*tek*, 3rd personal pronoun, *-ka*, accusative suffix); *id-gille* 'to you' (*ir*, 2nd personal pronoun, *-gille*, dative suffix); *yas-s-ana* 'they knew' (*yar-*, 'to know,' *-s*, past tense suffix); *paynna* 'he writes' (*pay-*, 'to write,' *-r*, imperfective aspect suffix); *id-mē* 'you are' (*ir*, 2nd sg. personal pronoun, *-mē*, focal-modal suffix).

(3) The nasal /n/ totally assimilates to the liquids, the sibilant /s/, the nasal /m/, and partially (according to place of articulation) to the affricate /j/: *deñj-* 'to give (something)' (*den-*, 'to give,' *-j*, transitive suffix); *mis-s-e* 'I was not' (*min-* 'not to be,' *-s*, past tense suffix, *-e*, 1st sg. ending); *im-min-e-so* 'do not be!' (*in-*, 'to be,' *min-*, negative suffix).

Progressive assimilation

16 (1) Two liquids in contact are solved with progressive assimilation: *dul-l-ana* 'they are, they remain' (*dul-*, 'to be, remain,' *-r*, imperfective aspect suffix); *ukur-ro* 'in the day' (*ukur* 'day,' *-lo*, locative-ablative suffix).

(2) In some cases the lateral liquid may not be totally assimilated to the vibrant: *diarió* 'in death' (*diar* 'death,' *-lo*, locative-ablative suffix).

(3) The nasal /n/ is assimilated to the liquids: *miššanno* 'in all' (*miššan-* 'everything,' *-lo*, locative-ablative suffix); *min-n-e* 'I am not' (*min-* 'not to be,' *-r*, imperfect aspect suffix).

In ON texts it happens quite often that some of the letters which should undergo the foregoing rules of assimilation remain unchanged. There are two possible explanations: either the assimilation was not applied for whatever reason or the scribe deemed it unnecessary to mark.

17   Other phonetic processes which are worth mentioning include root vowel alternation, for which it is impossible to describe a set of consistent patterns:

- a/i: ŋal-/ŋil- 'to see,' kap-/kip- 'to eat'
- u/i: dutrap/ditrap 'fowl'
- o/u: on-/un- 'to love,' kon-/kun- 'to have'
- e/i: et-/it- 'to grasp,' el-/il- 'to find'

	Bilabial		Dental		Palatal		Velar	
	vl	vd	vl	vd	vl	vd	vl	vd
Stops	p		t	d			k	g
Affr.					j			
Fric.		w				y		
Lat.						l		
Nas.		m		n		ñ		ŋ
Vibr.						r		
Sib.			s		š			

Table 2
Old Nubian consonants.

	Front	Central	Back
High	ī/i		ū/u
Mid	ē/e		ō/o
Low		ā/a	

Table 3
Old Nubian vowels.

18   The ON syllable can be of two types: CV and CVC. As said before, hiatus is avoided by inserting a laryngeal sound (in the opinion of B. Stricker [57, pp. 440–41], the intervocalic dot should be viewed as the glottal obstruent /'/). The dot also appears on vowels beginning a word, though not always. It can be assumed that cases where the dot is not marked are due exclusively to graphic considerations. Neither clusters of three consonants in morpheme boundary, nor clusters of two consonants at the beginning or the end of the word were al-

lowed. In those cases the consonant cluster was avoided by inserting the epenthetic vowel /i/. There are only a couple of exceptions where three-consonant clusters may be found: *darpne* 'donation, offering,' *pirgne* 'vegetables.' It is possible that in those cases some vowels were involved, but that they were graphically not represented. There are some phonetic restrictions at the beginning and the end of the word: a word cannot begin with the liquids and the nasals /n/ and /ñ/. The word can end only in vowels, /l/ and /n/ (for examples involving the epenthetic vowel at the beginning of the word, see section "Lexicon," as for epenthesis at the end of the word, see section "Morphology").

The derivation of nouns may result in stems with either an open or a closed syllable. The stem of derived verbs always has a closed syllable. The derivative verbal suffix may consist of one or two consonants or be made of one closed syllable. Similar peculiarities can be observed in the case of naturalized Greek verbal loanwords (see section "Lexicon").

Lexicon

19 All word classes of the inherited (Nubian) vocabulary are well represented in ON texts. While there is a significant percentage of borrowings among nouns, there are only exceptional cases among verbs.

20 ON nominal bases may be simple, derived, or compounded.

Simple nominal bases are almost always monosyllabic, which agrees with the monosyllabicity of ON morphemes. They have the following structures:

- V: *i* 'man,' *i* 'hand';
- VC: *uk* 'day,' *ag* 'mouth';
- CV: *ŋa* 'son,' *taa* 'girl';
- CVC: *sal* 'word,' *ŋoog* 'house.'

In texts one can apparently find disyllabic nominal bases made of two simple monosyllabic bases (*kumpu* 'egg'). It is possible that we have here a derived base. However, we do not have at our disposal enough textual material to divide the base into primary base and derived suffix. Polysyllabic non-derived noun bases may be loanwords that have been naturalized as if they were non-derived bases: *artosi* 'bread for offerings,' from Greek *ártos* 'bread'; *emente* 'underworld,' from Coptic *emĕnte*.

21 Derived noun bases may be disyllabic or trisyllabic, very rarely monosyllabic. They consist of a base to which one or two derivative suffixes have been attached. These suffixes, in isolation, are the following:

Table 4. Nominal suffixes

1. -e	9. -al	17. -itt(i)	
2. -o	10. -as	18. -att(i)	
3. -r (-ar, -er, -ir, -or, -ur)	11. -is	19. -katt(i)	
4. -t	12. -ko	20. -ide	
5. -ki	13. -kad	21. -kane	
6. -ig	14. -te	22. -kante	
7. -it	15. -ne		
8. -an	16. -der		

As for the latter two suffixes, we can isolate a basic monosyllabic suffix plus the element *-kan (cf. the same element in enkan 'or').

There are only two bases to be referred to as compounded noun bases: itmon 'hater of men, misanthrope,' from it 'man' and mon- 'to hate' and garkemso '(the four corners of the) world,' from gar 'side' and kemso 'four.'

22 ON verbal bases are divided into simple non-derived, simple derived, reduplicated, and compounded.

Simple non-derived bases are usually monosyllabic. They have the following structures:

- V: i- 'to say, speak';
- VV: aw- 'to do';
- VC: ag- 'to sit,' ir- 'to know';
- CV: ko- 'to have,' pi- 'to be, lay, remain';
- CVC: dul- 'to be,' par- 'to write,' mid- 'to run';
- VCC: ulg- 'to hear,' ank- 'to remember';
- CVCC: tank- 'to fulfill.'

It cannot be said with full confidence that we have something like disyllabic non-derived bases or just derived bases, since there is not enough textual evidence to segment them. We can notice borrowed verbal bases among the disyllabic non-derived bases: silel- 'to pray' (from Coptic šlēl); pistew- 'to believe' (from Greek pistéuō).

There is but only a handful of derivative suffixes that allows the creation of derived verbal bases from both verbal and nominal bases. They include:

1. The inchoative suffix -ŋ, (variants -iŋ, -aŋ, or -oŋ): dawaŋ- 'to augment, increase,' from dawu 'big, great'; dullaŋ- 'to become,' from dul- 'to be.'

2. The stative suffix -*en* (possible from the verb *en*- 'to be'): *itten*- 'to be a woman,' from *itt* 'woman'; *werēn*- 'to be one thing, a whole,' from *wer* 'one.'
3. The causative suffix -*gir*, -*tir*, -*kir*, and -*gar* (it has a non-syllabic variant between vowels, i.e., -*gr*, -*tr*, -*kr*): *unnatir*- 'to make give birth,' from *unn*- 'to give birth'; *yarilgir*- 'to get known (a woman),' from *yar*- 'to know'; *pilligir*- 'to illuminate, discover,' from *pill- 'to light,' *ŋoktir*- 'to glorify,' from *ŋok* 'fame, glory.'

23 Reduplicated bases come without exception from the doubling of non-derived bases. This conveys the meaning of iterativity (or intensity): *pipi*- 'to be insistent,' from *pi*- 'to be, remain'; *pajipajigir*- 'to test constantly,' from *paj*- 'to test'; *gelgeltak*- 'to roll away.'

24 Compounded bases are always the result of joining two verbal bases: *koju*- 'to take with itself,' from *ko*- 'to have' and *ju*- 'to go'; *sewit*- 'to inherit,' from *sew*- 'to follow' and *it*- 'to take.' The second element becomes a verbal derivative suffixes after it has lost its lexical content (grammaticalization). For example, the stative verbal suffix -*en* is written exactly like the verb *en*- 'to be,' from which it most likely is derived.

25 Apart from the inherited lexicon, ON shows also borrowed lexicon, being limited almost exclusively to the noun domain.

During its entire history, the fate of Nubia has been linked to the neighboring Ethiopia, and in the early Middle Age, Nubia had very intense cultural contacts with Byzantium (as medieval chronicles tell us, the Nubian empire was Christianized by missionaries sent by Constantine the Great). It is a recognized fact that during the period when the ON texts known to us today were translated and written down, Greek and Coptic literatures were widely spread. Additionally, according to the testimony of one Arabic historian, in Nubia people also wrote in Syriac.

Taking into account all this, and leaving apart the inherited lexicon, two different layers of borrowings may be distinguished in the composition of the ON vocabulary: Greek (this is the most extensive) and Coptic-Egyptian. In ON there is no evidence of Arabian loanwords, unlike in modern Nubian dialects, where they are very numerous.

Researchers have identified in the ON texts about 15 Coptic-Egyptian loanwords and more than 30 Greek loanwords (about a 6% of all the ON known vocabulary):

1. Words expressing Christian concepts: *istawrosi*, from Greek *staurós* 'cross'; *martyrosi*, from Greek *mártyros* 'martyr';
2. Words related to Church life and ritual: *igon*, from Greek *eikṓn* 'image, icon'; *psall-*, from Greek *psállō* 'to sing, hymn';
3. Abstract-religious and philosophical concepts: *pistew-*, from Greek *pistéwō* 'to believe'; *kosmosi*, from Greek *kósmos* 'world, universe'; *emente*, from Coptic *emĕnte* 'underworld';
4. Names of periods of time: *suáy* 'month,' from Coptic (Bohairic) *suai* 'first of the month'; *kyriake*, from Greek *kyriakē̄* 'Sunday';
5. Some words are loanwords from Old Egyptian and Coptic dealing with cultural and daily life objects: *orpi*, from Old Egyptian *irp*, Coptic *ērp* 'wine'; or *šo-l*, from Old Egyptian *šōr* 'book' (Demotic *šʿ.t*).

Judging from the texts, Coptic loanwords entered ON almost without a change. Greek words entered with total or partial adaptation. Virtually all nouns and adjectives adopted the form of the nominative singular which was interpreted as the ON base. Two verbal bases borrowed from Greek were adopted partially (without the vowel person ending). The obvious explanation for this is that the ON derived verbal base (i.e., polysyllabic) ends in a closed syllable, so that Greek verbal stems are adapted according to this model. The adaptation of loanwords took place according to ON phonotactics: hiatus is broken by means of a sound, marked with the intervocalic dot; consonant clusters in *Inlaut* and *Auslaut* are both avoided with epenthetic /i/ (see examples in section "Nouns").

Loanwords follow ON paradigms and derivations: participle *pistewolgu* 'believing, that believes' from the verb *pistew-* 'to believe' (Greek *pistéuō*); the verb *árkhiéreósaŋ* 'to be a high priest' from the noun *árkhiéreósi* 'high priest' (Greek *archieréus*).

In addition to this, it has been suggested that there is a certain amount of Meroitic [Mer.] loanwords in the ON lexicon: *mašal*, from Mer. *maše* 'sun'; *wiñji*, from Mer. *wayeki* 'star'; *jem* or *gem*, from Mer. *gemi* 'year.' Also the verb *ir-* 'to give birth to' may be included here. It can be assumed from certain derivatives and some titles that these words arrived into ON from Old Egyptian via Meroitic. This conclusion would also account for the layer of Meroitic loanwords (or from other languages genetically related to ON).

Morphology

26 ON is of the agglutinative type. The most important grammatical mechanism is suffixation. It is possible that in earlier stages, previous to the fixation of the texts, in ON there were also prefixes. The rudimentary prefix *m- expressing negation might bear witness of that stage, cf. on- 'to love' vs. mon- 'to hate'; irkane 'birth' vs. mira 'barren.'

The following six word classes can be distinguished: 1) noun, 2) pronoun, 3) numerals, 4) verb, 5) interjections, 6) postpositions and particles, and 7) the word cluster. As categories, the last two classes occupy the intermediate position: postpositions are to be described as elements between the morpheme and the word, and the word cluster, between the word and a combination of words.

Noun

27 ON nouns may present the following maximal template: base + derivative suffix + plural suffix + determiner + case ending (+ focal or modal particle).

The minimal template looks as follows: root + case ending.

28 ON nouns distinguish number, case, and possession. There is no gender in ON.

29 Number: singular has no formal expression whereas plural is expressed by the suffix -gu: ukrigu 'days' (from uk(u)r 'day'). Before this suffix, the animated and unanimated markers -ri and -ni can be attached: apostolosrïgu 'apostles' (from Greek apóstolos 'apostle'); dogdrigu 'magi' (see Modern Nubian dogir 'magician,' 'water spirit'); kissenigu 'churches' (from kisse); saïtengu 'olives' (from *saïte). However, the use of one or another suffix is sometimes unclear: together with apostolosrïgu we can find even apostolosgu 'apostles.'

There are a couple of examples involving the analytic expression of the dual number (for body parts) with the help of the genitive -(i)n singular and the element -tri: mañin-tri 'eyes,' ȯen-tri 'legs.'

Suppletive number marking is also attested: itt 'woman' pl. iliwgu (M) or iltigu (PC).

In case the noun has the plural suffix, then the determiner suffix follows it. If the noun is in singular, the determiner suffix precedes derivative suffixes. The determiner suffix carries out the function of a determining article. With vowel ending stems the determiner suffix is directly added: watto-l 'everything,' kisse-l 'the church,' so-l 'the book.' With consonant ending stems, the epenthetic vowel /i/ is inserted between the stem and the determiner suffix: ŋok-i-l from ŋok 'glory,' kosmos-i-l 'the world, the universe' (from Greek kósmos).

30 There are different opinions among researchers about the status of the case endings in ON. The majority of suffixes, with the exception of the case endings, are labeled "postpositions." However, in contradistinction to genuine postpositions which clearly are joined to a regular nominal base, all case morphemes follow after the determiner suffix or, if the noun is in plural, precedes the plural suffix. Analysis of the texts, especially the Lectionary which can be compared with the original version in Greek, allows us to distinguish nine cases:

(1) Nominative has zero-ending: watto 'everything,' ŋal 'son.' In the case of consonant-final stems, which are phonetically inadmissible, the epenthetic vowel /i/ surfaces, for example, after the last consonant: kosmosi (from Greek kósmos) 'world'; after geminated consonants in Auslaut: till-i 'God.'

(2) Due to its special status, it is worth noting the absolutive case. It is expressed by the suffix -a: ŋokkor-a 'miracle,' pap-a 'father,' Emmanuel-a 'Emmanuel.'

After the plural marker -gu, the absolutive case ending adopts the form -e. In many instances this allomorph is followed by the particle -ke: ágoppeguė(-ma) '(you are) the helmsman' (PC, I, 9); ontakraguė-ke 'beloved' (PC, I, 6, see also other texts). In the particular case of pap 'father,' the absolutive case carries out the function of vocative: papo 'Father!' (Jn., 4, 10).

(3) The genitive function is carried out by the suffix -na or -(i)n: kyriaken 'of Sunday,' ted-i-n 'of the law,' jel-gu-na 'of the times.' The difference between these two variants is based on the vocalic apophony of the base, that is, whether the base has reduced or full grade vocalism. The very same distinction is also found among some verbal endings (vid. infra).

(4) The accusative suffix is -ka: wiñji-ka 'star,' tak-ka 'him,' pawu-ka 'power.' Sometimes it can be possible to find a reduced variant of this suffix, for example, before a following vowel: ŋak'-ende ask'-ende 'neither a son nor a daughter' (M, 3).

(5) The dative marker is -gil or the free variant -gille: aygil 'to me,' targille 'to him,' igongille 'to the image, icon.'

(6) In ON it is possible to identify the inessive case: -la (variants -iá after vowels or -r). It expresses movement inside of a closed space. By "closed space" we refer to:

- man, his heart, or his thoughts: aya 'in me,' teriá 'in them,' ayl-la 'in the heart';
- buildings, locations: ŋog-la 'at home,' kisse-la 'in the church,' dipp-u-wel-la 'in a village';
- the world: kosmos-la 'in the world.'

Sometimes the inessive expresses movement towards the inside or the outside of something: kisse-ŋiss-la 'into the holy church,' ted-gu-la 'out from the laws.'

(7) Locative case expresses external location, basically in open spaces. The locative suffix is -lo (the variant -ió appears after vowels and -r, after consonants -no). By "open spaces" we refer to:

- inhabited places: bithlémi-iudayn-no 'in the Jewish Bethlehem';
- cardinal points: mašalosk-lo 'in the East';
- periods of time: ukri-gu-lo 'in days,' tawka-miššan-no 'at any time' (lit. 'time-any-in').

The locative is also figuratevly used to express abstract concepts: ale-lo 'indeed.'

As happens with the inessive case, the locative may carry out nuances proper of the ablative (external separation) or the allative (external direction towards): kisse-lo '(she left) to(wards) the church,' but also '(yes indeed he will be excommunicated) from the church.'

(8) There are traces also of a superessive case, expressed by the marker -do: iskit-i-l-do 'on the earth,' kul-i-d-d-o 'on the mountain.' This case may also express abstract concepts: istawrosil-do teylgu 'those who trust on the Cross' (lit. 'on the Cross the trusting ones'), ted-do silela 'having prayed for them' (lit. 'for them having prayed').

There is one single instance of the superessive expressing movement from up to down with the suffix -don: harmi-don 'up from the sky.'

(9) Lastly, the comitative case, expressed by the suffix *-dal: psal-lilgul-dal* 'with the ones who celebrate,' *ay-dal* 'with me,' *ur-jimmil-gu-l-dal* 'with all of us.'

For a more detailed description of the case functions, see section "Case function" (§60.1–4).

Pronouns

31 ON distinguishes three different pronominal bases: personal, demonstrative, and interrogative.

32 (1) We know the full set of personal pronouns (there are attested two different forms for the 1PL that the specialists call "inclusive," i.e., "we, including you" and "exclusive," i.e., "we, excluding you"). The bases of these pronouns have the following shape:

Table 4
Personal pronouns.

	SG	PL
1	*ay* 'I'	*u* 'we' (INCL) / *er* 'we' (EXCL)
2	*ir* 'thou'	*ur* 'you'
3	*tar* 'he/she/it'	*ter* 'they'

Personal pronouns are treated as nouns, this means they can receive case endings and be followed by postpositions: *takka* 'him,' *aygil* 'to me,' *targille* 'to him,' *teriá* 'in them,' *irio-tjo* 'on you,' *eddal* 'with us,' *urió-joá* 'about you.' Personal pronouns, in contradistinction with nouns, have no zero-ending for the nominative, but the suffix *-u*: *uru* 'you.'

(2) Possessive pronouns are directly taken from the reduced grade of the genitive form (rarer from the full grade form): *anna* or *an* 'my,' *inna* or *in* 'your,' *tanna* or *tan* 'his/her/its,' *unna* or *un* 'our (inclusive),' *enna* or *en* 'our,' *unna* (or **un*) 'your' (the short variant is not attested), *ten* (or **tenna*) 'their' (the full grade variant is not attested).

(3) *apo* 'my father' contains what evidently is a prefixed pronoun. This form may be pointing to the fact that some personal pronouns in ON could have functioned as possessive pronouns, as happens in modern Nubian dialects.

33 Forms carrying out the function of reflexive pronouns are expressed by adding the reflexive marker *-ono* to the corresponding accusative form of the personal pronoun *ayk-ono* 'myself,' *takk-ono* 'himself, by his own.'

34 We are aware of two demonstrative pronouns: *in* 'this' is used for near objects, and for far objects *man* 'that.' Demonstrative pronouns create a word cluster together with the determined word: *in-šol* 'this book,' *in-ted-gu* 'these laws,' *man-dippi-la* 'in that city,' *man-itt-i-l* 'that woman.'

In those cases when the demonstrative stands alone, it is declined according to case and number as with nouns: *inka* or *ininka* 'this' (ACC), *iningu-la* 'in these' (inessive PL), *man-i-n* 'of that' (GEN), *min-in-gu* 'those' (NOM.PL).

35 There are three interrogative pronouns attested in ON: *is* 'who,' *min* 'what,' and *ŋai* 'who; what,' plus the interrogative element *mna* 'what, or,' possibly a derivative of the pronoun *min*. The rest of interrogative notions are expressed with the cases and postpositions of two pronouns: *is-gil* 'to where' (dative), *is-lo* 'where' (locative), *minga* 'what (do you want)' (ACC), *ŋaeia* 'how' (inessive), plus the postpositional construction: *juri-min-no-jun* 'why, by virtue of what reason?' (lit. 'reason-what-in-to').

36 (1) The function of the indefinite pronoun is carried out by the numeral *wer ~ wel* 'one,' with which the determined word forms a word cluster (see M, 2): *itt-u-wel-lo* 'a woman,' *dipp-u-wel-la* 'in a village or settlement.'

(2) The reciprocal pronoun is expressed by reduplicating the indefinite *wer*: *werwek-ka* 'one to another,' *wėrwel-dal* 'with one to another.'

Numerals

37 In ON, numbers were usually written with Greek numerical signs, that is, letters of the alphabet with a diacritic: *gem* 'year,' *gem-u-IB* '12 years,' *gem-u-IG* '13 years,' or *ΧΠΘ* (Greek) '(year) 689 (of the Martyrs)' (Coptic calendar, corresponding to the year 973).

But numerals written in words sometimes can be found (these are most of times numbers of the first decade).

38 (1) We are aware of the following ordinal numbers:

- *wer* (or *wel*) 'one'
- *wo(l)* 'two'
- *tusko* 'three'

- *kemso* 'four'
- *dij* 'five'
- *koloti* 'seven'
- *idwi* 'eight'
- *irkisigu* 'forty'
- *dude* 'thousand'
- *tituu...* 'ten thousand'

As is only natural, all the numbers belonging to the decade series carry the plural suffix. There is a single instance of a number belonging to the decade series written symbolically (but the plural suffix is still required): *p̄-igu* 'eighty.'

The ordinal number and the countable word form a word cluster (*vid. infra*).

39 There are some cardinal numbers attested in the text of the Apocalypse: *tuskantel* 'first' (derived from *tuskante* 'beginning'), *wel* 'second.' There are two formations that have been derived with the help of the suffix *-it* (*-ti*): *tuskitti* 'third,' *kolotitka* 'seventh' (Apoc., VIII. 1–8; XIV. 8–9).

40 To all appearances, the adverbial suffix *-an* also served as multiplicative suffix. It was added to the corresponding ordinal number: *weran* 'once,' *kolotan* 'seven times.'

41 There are nouns derived from the ordinal number *tusko* 'three' with the help of the derivative suffix *-it*: *tusk-it* 'the Trinity.'

Verb

42 The ON verb distinguishes person, number, consecutive (subjunctive) mood, time, aspect, and voice.

43 Verb personal endings differ from the rest of ON morphemes in that they show different meanings. While each ON morpheme expresses one and only one grammeme (inflectional or derivational meaning), as is the case with languages of the agglutinative type, each verb personal ending expresses three grammemes: person, number, and subjunctivity. Personal endings of the absolutive verbal forms are the following (simple predicate):

	SG	PL
1	-e	-o
2	-na	-o
3	-na	-ana

Table 5
Personal endings of simple predicates.

The set of personal endings which are used in consecutive verbal formations (complex predicates) can be characterized as "narrowed" variants of the personal endings in absolutive verbal formations. They differ in terms of zero-grade vs. full-grade vowel, or short form vs. full form, respectively.

	SG	PL
1	-i	-u
2	-(i)n	-u
3	-(i)n	-an

Table 6
Personal endings of complex predicates.

44 Modality is expressed by means of (a) suffixes which are attached directly to the preceding personal ending, or (b) particles. In ON it is possible to distinguish four moods: indicative, imperative, conditional, and subjective (the subjective mood in complex sentences is expressed not by suffixes, but by particles).

The indicative mood has zero-ending. All tenses are available in the indicative mood (vid. infra for the conjugation of all tenses in the indicative mood).

The imperative mood has its own set of personal endings: -e and -ana (for 2SG and 2PL). As a rule, imperative forms are followed by the particle -so: awlos-e '(thou) be safe,' piss-e-so '(thou) be glad!,' awij-ana-so '(you) do!,' pes-aï-so '(you) speak!' (rarer variant of the plural ending).

The 1PL form -am-so is also attested: untika konam-so : tokonnaweka duam-so (C, 13) 'let us have love, let us wish peace.'

G.M. Browne mentions that the negative form of the imperative has the marker -tamē, e.g., aēttaka-tamē (M, 22) '(woman) do not be anxious!,' kippa-tamē (PC, 21, 21; 22, 7) '(thou) do not eat!' It is possible that this marker comes from the subjective mood -mē and the element -ta. The latter is allegedly preserved in the negative form of the verb eir- 'to can, be able': eirimentalo (Mth., V, 14) '(it) cannot.' These markers are added to the converb in -a.

The underlined conditional mood is expressed by the marker -*ko* and it is used in the conditional and purposive clauses. It is sometimes accompanied by also by the particle -*lo* or -*lon*. Only 3SG and 3PL forms are attested: *ilen-ko-n* 'he speaks-if,' *kendukki-kaw-an-no* 'they make a donation-if' (-*kaw* is a rare variant of the conditional mood marker).

The subjective mood is expressed with the help of either particles (see section "Postpositions and particles") or the suffix -*imm*. It is used to express wishes, future plans, and in direct speech. The subjective mood suffix -*imm* goes back, obviously, to the suffix -*m*, whose in origin may be the same subjective particle, and the imperfective aspect -*r*, which precedes and to which is assimilated. Future and present forms of the subjuctive mood are attested with the full form of the personal endings (in subordinate sentences the subjective mood is always expressed by a particle).

Present tense (1SG & PL): *ŋalid-imm-e* 'I want to see,' *doll-imm-o* 'we want that....'

Future tense (1SG, 3SG & PL): *gallatidd-imm-e* 'I shall reveal' (direct speech within a sentence), *edd-imm-a* 'shall receive' (direct speech), *unnad-imm-ana* 'let them give birth.'

45 In ON the indicative mood has four tenses: present, simple past, anterior, and future. Tense markers immediately precede the personal endings which may appear in their full or reduced forms.

(1) Present tense seems to have zero-ending. The imperfective suffix -*r* appears with all persons, but 3SG and 2SG, where it is lost. It seems characteristic of it that it is lost after consonants (3SG and 2SG have personal endings, beginning with a consonant). Almost all forms of the present tense are attested with both full and short variants of the personal endings.

    1SG: *ki-r-e* 'I come,' *men-e-r-i* 'I am not'
    2SG: *dawi-na* 'you are great'
    3SG: *oktak-na* 'he is named,' *aruán-ïn* 'he waters'
    1PL: *egid-r-u* 'we inquire, ask'
    2PL: *in-n-o* '(you) are,' *ekid-r-u* 'you inquire, ask'
    3PL: *in-n-ana* 'they are' (from **in-r-ana*), *kip-r-an* 'they eat'

(2) The simple past tense is marked with the suffix -*s*. Simple past is attested as part of both simple and complex sentences. When used in subordinate clauses, this tense expresses that that action is completed in relation to the event described in the main clause. Almost all forms of the simple past tense are attested.

1SG: *eski-s-e* 'I conquered,' *tijje-s-i* 'I gave'
2SG: *denji-s-na* 'you gave (me),' *one-s-in* 'you beloved'
3SG: *itir-s-na* 'he sent,' *unnu-s-in* 'she gave birth'
1PL: *kas-s-o* 'we came'
2PL: *égidi-s-u* 'we inquired, asked'
3PL: *yas-s-ana* 'they knew,' *awij-s-an* 'they did'

There is attested only one case of analytic use, where the role of auxiliary verb is played by *in-* 'to be': *ŋili-kon inise* (Apoc. VIII, 2; XIV, 14) 'and I saw' (lit. 'saw-and-was').

In some cases the imperfective aspect suffix *-r* appears in front of the simple past tense marker so that the simple past tense acquires imperfect value: *mayka-a-r-i-s-na* 'she was ashamed.'

If the action of the main clause is expressed with simple past, the simple past form in the subordinate clause acquires past perfect (pluperfect) value: *kosmosla-gil ayk etrésin-kello. ay tekka kosmosla-gil itasse* (Jn., XVII, 18) 'as you sent me to the world, I had sent them to the world' (lit. to-world-me(-you)-sent-as, I them to-world sent).

If the main clause predicate contains the future tense, the past tense in the dependent clause has the meaning of "past in the future": *ay-on kumpu-tuskan telo-unnusin-ka-lo tan kissela utuddre* (M, 9) '(...) I will donate to his church (i.e., Saint Mena's) the egg that it has first laid' (lit. 'I-and egg-in-beginning-(she-)-gave-birth-to-it his into-church make-a-donation').

(3) The anterior tense has the suffix *-o* (in 3PL *-u*). It describes an action which takes place before the main action. The anterior is only attested in a type of subordinate clause: the temporal subordinate clause, and only if the action of the main clause is rendered with the simple past: *ukrigul ŋoka-joruan-non... kisana* (M, 36) 'when the days of (three months) had gone by, they came' (lit. days passed-and... they came). The anterior here plays also the role of a temporal, referential intermediary between the action of the main clause and the action of the subordinate clause.

In simple predicates, if the context has present tense, the anterior may correspond to the simple past or have a resultative meaning: *diyk-on koá-lo énona. sewattk-on konmenna-lo* (M, 4-5) 'She acquired a lot (...), (but) she did not have a heir' (lit. many-having-was, successor-GEN not-has).

If the context has past tense, the anterior may correspond to the past perfect (pluperfect) along with the additional resultative meaning: *ŋawira... l-appa akdaktakari... in-de ŋissa-lo pestakona* (Heb., IX, 2) 'The tabernacle having been set up in the first [room]... and it was called the "Holy [Place]"' (lit. tabernacle... for she-set up... that-and holy was-called) (the original Greek has present tense).

If future should be understood from the context, the anterior tense may express an action that follows next. The relation of determinability is retained, although inverted: *ikarigra-lo iśrāili-watto ŋartakkona* (Rom., XI, 26) ('...until the full number of the Gentiles has come in.) And in this way the entire Israel shall escape' (lit. 'so- and Israel-entire shall-escape').

(4) In ON there are two different variants of the future tense marker: *-d* (*-de, -di*) and *-arr*. Suffix *-d* appears when the verb base ends with a consonant or the liquids *r, l*: *ŋokordre* (PC, 1, 12–13) 'I shall admire'; *idinne* (ibid., 6) 'I will tell'; *ŋuruddna* (St., 20) 'he will embower'; *kedadoddna* (St., 23) 'he will rise.'

Suffix *-arr* appears after verb bases ending with a vowel or a vowel complex: *paskarre* 'I shall punish,' *awarrinna* 'he is going to do.'

If the main clause predicate has present tense, the future tense in the dependent clause is used with its fully proper meaning: *dollimmo uka-yarilgadjaden-ka... mystirka* (St., 12) 'We want you reveal the secret to us' (lit. 'we want-let us-you reveal-ACC... the secret').

If the action of the main clause is expressed with a past form, the future tense of the subordinate clause carries out the function of "future in the past": *ittil-lon pessna ale-sin inno tukren isgil jodin* (M, 14) 'And the woman said: "Truly, when you depart from here, where will you go?"' (lit. 'woman-and said indeed from-this departing where he-goes'). This is the only example which bears witness of an indirect question where the predicate has a short form of the personal ending.

If the main clause predicate has future tense, it means that the future tense in the subordinate describes an action simultaneous to the action of the main clause, i.e., it overlaps with the fully proper meaning of the future tense: *kosmos-wattoka peššajeri-lo istawros-u-ŋokkol-lon ŋonjanna* (St., 18) 'when I will judge the entire world, the holy Cross... shall stand' (lit. 'world-entire I-will-judge-and cross-holy... shall stand').

46 In ON there are two voices: active and reflexive-passive. There is no special passive conjugation. The reflexive-passive voice is marked by the suffix *-tak*: *unn-* 'to give birth' → *unn-u-tak-* 'to be born,' *pes-* 'to speak' → *pes-tak-* 'to be said, named; to be spoken.'

If the subject does not require a direct object, then the active voice has no marker. In case it does, the verb takes the transitive ending: suffix *-r* in case the direct object is singular, but suffix *-j* if the direct object is plural: *pes-* 'to speak' → *pes-ir-* or *pes-ij-* 'to say something' (if direct speech follows), *ėgid-, ėkid-* 'to ask, inquire' → *ėkidru ayka* (St., 10) 'you ask me,' *tekka ėgid-j-i-s-na* (Mth., II, 4) '(he) asked them.'

The ON verb hereby requires subject–object agreement.

The origin of the reflexive-passive voice suffix -*tak* is, to all appearances, not verbal. Evidently, it derives from the short form of the 3SG personal pronoun accusative: *tak* (this suffix has been alternatively written as *takka* once, cf. the full form: *takka*).

47 After the voice suffix follows the suffix of negation, -*men* or -*min* (from the verb *en*- 'to be' and the original negation prefix *m-): *psall*- 'to hymn' → *psall-i-men*- 'not to hymn,' *pes*- 'to say' → *pes-min*- 'not to say.' When used as a lexical morpheme, it means 'to be not.'

In ON the negation is adverbial.

48 The non-finite formations are created also from the verbal base. There are seemingly two types of derived forms: participles and infinitives, which are used to create the non-finite formations: converbs (lit. "gerunds," there are two kinds: coordinative and subordinative) and supines (also two kinds).

(1) The ON <u>participle</u> is formed from verbal bases (with or without the aspect and tense markers). The element -*l* is attached to the base. Participles, like nouns, are inflected for number and case. Obviously, the element -*l* does not play here the role of article, but of the participle suffix. In case the participle must appear as defined, then the article (i.e., another element -*l*) is added: *psall-i-l-gu-l* 'the ones who hymn.' Participles may carry out the function of subject (in nominative), direct or indirect object, circumstantial (in the oblique cases and in postpositional constructions), and complement (in genitive).

Participles have present, simple past and future tense. Present has zero ending: *añ-i-l* 'living, that lives' from *añ*- 'to live.' Simple past usually has the anterior suffix -*o* before the participle element -*l*, the anterior suffix -*s* being less frequent: *pestak-o-l* 'said' from *pestak*- 'be said,' *kip-s-i-l* 'eaten' from *kip*- 'to eat.' Future has the same future tense marker before the participle element -*l*: *pes-a-d-ik-ka* 'what will say' (from *pes*- 'to speak').

There are aspectual distinctions: present participle expresses simultaneous action relative to the main verb, past participle expresses anteriority, and future participle, consecutiveness.

(2) The second derived form is the <u>infinitive</u> (verbal noun). The infinitive is obtained from the verbal base, without tense or aspect markers, by adding the suffix -*e*. As a verbal noun, the infinitive may take the place of a different sentence constituent as well as function as the logic predicate in infinitive phrases: *in ayk itreka* (Jn., XVII, 23), lit. 'your me sending,' from the original Greek *hóti sỳ mè apésteilas* 'what you sent me.'

(3) The coordinative converb essentially appears after the absolutive form of the participle. The determiner -*l* is absent here, as far as it cannot stand with the noun in the absolutive case (this follows from the function of the absolutive case as the case of a formally non-determined sentence constituent). The coordinative converb may function as a regular noun in the absolutive case (see section "Case Functions"), as a nominal predicate or the equivalent of a participle used in addressing words, cf. GEN in *tillik-un-nol-Marian* 'Saint (lit. 'God-begetteth' [Browne's Theotokos]) Mary' and ABS in addressing words: *tillik-unnara Maria* (M, 43–44) '(oh) Our Lady (lit. God-begetteth) Mary!.'

The coordinative gerund basically serves as the predicate in gerund phrases and it has a logic coordinative link with the main clause: *tan wiñjika mašalosklo ŋa-sin kasso-sin* (Mth., II, 2) 'We left for we saw His star in the East...' (lit. 'star in-the-East seeing-for (we) left-for').

If the gerund describes an uncompleted action relative to the action of the main clause, it takes the imperfective marker -*r* (variant -*ar*). If the converb with this marker carries out the function of predicate in dependent clauses, the action expressed by it has an imperfective meaning: *utt-u-wel-lo dipp-u-wella du-ȧr-a* (M, 1) 'A woman was in a village; *tar-u-ŋodis-sin pes-i-r-a* (C, 43) 'For he, the Lord, said.'

(4) The subordinative gerund always carries out the same function: it is the logic predicate in dependent clauses, linked by a logic subordinative link with the main clause which can be temporal, conditional, or concessive. The marker -*en* is added to the bare verbal base, with no aspectual or temporal markers. For example, in a sentence containing *pes-en* 'speaking': *ale-sin weltril kika-pesen... kisselo pala-mē* (C, 5) 'For indeed, if someone speaks... yes, he will be excommunicated!' (lit. 'really-for someone speaking... from-church remove-let').

As is natural, the subordinative converb continues the genitive of the infinitive (infinitive marker -*e* + short form of the genitive suffix -*n*). This creates a clausal structure that equates the Classical Greek construction *genitivus absolutus*. A sentence where the logic subject stands in the full form of the genitive, and the logic predicate, in the short form of the genitive of the infinitive (or in the form of the subordinative converb?) is attested once: *enna werėnen* (Jn., XVII, 22) 'even as we are one' (lit. 'us the-one-being'). It is very likely that the subordinative converb comes from the *genitivus absolutus* construction: the subject, generally in the main clause, is omitted, and the logic predicate remains in the genitive.

The subordinative converb has a much rarer suffix: -*ken*. This suffix, as it can be inferred from not many instances, carries out the function of the predicate in concessive clauses: *it-wel... kenduk-ken... pesen* (C, 3) 'If some man, though bringing..., says' (or perhaps: 'when he shall bring' [?]) (lit. 'man-one... bringing... speaking...'). It is possible that this variant of the gerund comes from the genitive of certain verbal formations in *-ke*. Such formations, documented in the texts on few occasions, have the meaning of potentiality: *wėr-aŋ-i-men-ke-r-a-lo* (Mth., V, 13) 'it is good for nothing' (lit. 'one-be-come-not-possibly-to.be').

(5) The first supine is a verbal formation used as the logic predicate of final clauses. The supine is formed by adding the marker *-iniá* (SG) and *-inuá* (PL) to the verbal base. Possible variants: *-eniá* or *-niá*, and *-enuá* or *-nuá*. The supine marker may be segmented in three parts. The segment *-in* (or *-en*, *-n*), to all appearances, seems to be the unreduced or reduced form of the subordinative converb, from which the supine derives (cf. the predicate of final clauses, which is created with the conditional and a particle). Elements *-i* and *-u* are of course identical to the short form of the personal endings: 1SG *-i* and 1&2PL *-u*, respectively. But here they do not express three different grammemes, as happens with finite verbal formations, but only one, i.e., number. At last, *-a* is the subjunctive mood particle used in subordinate clauses (cf. section "Syntax"): *kimma sioniá-ketal awlel gipirt-en-i-á* (Rom., XI, 26) 'There shall come out of Sion the Deliverer, and shall turn away...' (lit. 'he.will.come-PRT from-Sion the-Savior turn-to'); *kasso-sin takka duku-n-u-á* (Mth., II, 2) 'For we... are come to worship him' (lit. 'we-came-you.see him kneel-to').

(6) We should mention still the second supine which occupies an intermediate position between finite and non-finite formations. It appears in the predicate of final clauses, where the logic subject of the main clause is carried out by the direct object. It is created with the imperative and the particle *-a*. If the imperative particle *-so* is used instead, it presents the truncated variant *-s*: *ósije-á-yon-seniminne-so* (Jn., XVII, 15) 'I do not pray (to you) that thou shouldest take them out' (lit. 'take.away-to not ask.for'); *ekka denjisa ŋiss-u-minan kissela tijjana-s-a* (M, 33) '(a woman) gave it to us, in order to take it away to the church of Saint Mena' (lit. 'us given Saint-Mena to-church give-to'; in Nubian the argument of the verb 'to give' is expressed with accusative).

Postpositions and Particles

49 Postpositions and particles occupy an intermediate position between lexical and connective morphemes: although there are no distinctive features that would make them stand out, postpositions and particles must be dealt with jointly as an independent word class.

50 The ON postpositions can be divided into case-governing and connective. Particles can be classified as either focal or modal.

Case-dependent postpositions combine with a noun plus definite article. They carry out the same function that the noun in the noun phrase. Formally, postpositions of this kind could be further divided into two groups: those that combine with the noun in genitive and those that combine with the noun in locative.

(1) The group governing the locative includes ten postpositions:

1. *-goyan* 'than, in comparison to': *tillilo-goyan dawina-ï* (C, 25) '(you are) more than God';
2. *-kalo* 'after': *inno-kalo* (from */in-lo-kalo/*) 'after that';
3. *-ko* 'according to, in accord to': *sallo-ko* 'according to the word';
4. *-oro* 'in, by': *irió-óro* 'at you';
5. *-tjo* 'from': *irió-tjo* 'from you';
6. *-tusu* 'to(wards), before': *ukurtlo-tusu* 'before the foundation';
7. *-joá* 'for, through, by means': *tillilo-joá* 'to God'; *papigulo-joá* 'for the sake of fathers';
8. *-jun* instrumental postposition: *igulo-jun* 'by people';
9. *-ŋarro* 'out(side of)' (attested only once): *kisselo-ŋarro* 'out of the church';
10. *-kiskillo* 'until': *kirello-kiskillo* 'until the coming, until he arrives.'

(2) The group governing genitive includes seven postpositions:

1. *-kegagrá* 'with regard to': *sewartin-kegagrá* 'regarding the spirit';
2. *-non* 'similar to': *pigitkoñjilguna-non* 'similar to, like luminaries.' Unlike other postposition governing genitive, this postposition is attested only with the full form of the genitive.
3. *-pawu* 'in time': *kien-pawu* 'at the time of coming';
4. *-pawuka* '(right up) to': *dien-pawuka* '(right up) to (one's) death';
5. *-tawklo* 'during in the course of': *duen-tawklo* 'during the sojourn';
6. *-tawo* 'under': *mašen-tawo* 'under the bushel';
7. *-juriá* 'about, because': *kosmosin-juriá* 'about the world'; *en-ŋeyn-juriá* 'due to that issue.'

(3) As far as their meaningful elements are concerned, the postpositions governing the genitive have been subject to fewer changes than the locative ones: most of times there is no doubt about their origins. Twice we find the genitive to be linked with the formations *-awla* and *-tula*. They both mean 'in(side).' It is unclear whether they

must be regarded as derivatives or postpositional constructions. On the other hand, some postpositions governing the locative (e.g., *-oro*) sometimes are used with noun bases as if they were cases. The comitative case *-dal* used as a postposition with a noun in the locative is attested once. All this allows us to suppose that the locative group might be originally older than the genitive group.

(4) Dative *-gil* (or *-gille*) sometimes is used as a postpostion with the noun in inessive. It is associated almost always to a particular use of the dative, the so-called dative of direction: *kosmosla-gil* 'to the world,' *harmila-gille* 'to the sky.'

51 Connective postpositions carry out the function of conjuctions. They might stand before any sentence constituent. The following connective postpositions appear regularly in texts:

1. *-abba* or *-appa* 'for, then': *pesil-appa* 'indeed, this who talks...';
2. *-de* 'and': *in-di* 'and this';
3. *-ende* or *-ende...-ende* 'neither... nor': *ŋak'-ende ask'-ende* (M, 3) 'neither a son nor a daughter'; *wel-ende* 'not even one';
4. *-kolo* 'also, too': *sewart-u-ŋissin-no-kolo* 'and in the name of the Holy Spirit too' (lit. 'spirit-to.the.holy-in-too');
5. *-kel* 'also, too' together with the postposition *-de*, before the enumeration: *tad-de-on-tan-ogil-de-tan-ŋad-de-tan-medju nig-ul-de-kek-ka* (M, 65) '(baptized) her, her husband, her son, and her servants' (lit. 'she-and-her-husband-and-her-son-and-her-slaves-and-also-ACC');
6. *-kello* 'like, as (well as)': *pesen-kello* 'as said' (lit. 'saying-like');
7. *-ketal* 'also, too': *ik-ketal* 'you too' (from *ir-ketal*);
8. *-enko* or *-lenko* 'but': *oktakol-enko* 'but the called';
9. *-lon* 'yes, but; indeed (parenthetical connector)': *ittil-lon pessna* (M, 14) 'and the woman said,' *ierusalmi-wattol-lon* (Mth., II, 3) '(Herod the king was troubled,) and all Jerusalem with him';
10. *-on* 'and, but; indeed.' It links two identical phrases or two clauses in context: *harmna-on iskitna* 'of the sky and earth,' *ter-on pessna* 'and he said';
11. *-sin* 'for': *eskise-sin* (Jn., XVII, 33) 'for I conquered.'

52 Focal particles are used before noun phrases. It marks noun phrase or rheme. Particle *-lo* marks both noun phrase and rheme. Particle *-li* marks only noun phrase and it is attested only with 1SG & 2SG. Particle *-ke* appears only when the referent of the subject is 2PL and other plural contexts.

53 Modal particles stand before noun or verbal phrases and exhibit the markers of the subjective mood. There are two: in the predicate of independent clauses (expressing wish, intention or direct speech). Particle -*ma* or -*mi*, -*m'* may sometimes appear in phrases containing the verb 'to call, name, be called.' The particle -*a* is used in subordinate clauses (final, indirect speech).

For a more detailed account on the functions of both focal and modal particles, see the section "Syntax."

Other Word Classes

54 There are several adverbs attested in the ON texts. They are formed with the suffixes -*al* and -*an*. It is possible to mention others such as *dumal* 'suddenly,' *takan* 'quickly,' *makan* 'thus, therefore,' or *kolotan* 'seven times,' which is derived from the corresponding numeral.

55 The interjection *ė* functions as vocative: *ė itta* 'oh woman!,' *ė an pidta* 'oh my friend,' *ė tota* 'oh son!.'

56 Additionally, in texts we can find the words *isin* and *eihi* 'behold, here it is': *isin dogdrïgul mašalosklȯ tara iėrusalmiȯ kisana* (Mth, II, 1) 'Behold, Magi from the East came to Jerusalem.'

Syntax

57 In spite of the agglutinative character of the ON language, it is possible to observe substantial elements of incorporation.

Word clusters occupy the intermediate position between the word and a combination of words. They are closed sets of words or phrases (with truncated, i.e., reduced or unreduced words), which form a unit as if they were just one word. According to the integrity (non-segmentability), word clusters can be divided into three types: homogeneous, peripheral, or nominalized.

(1) The homogeneous word cluster is formed by a group of similar clause constituents. All words in this complex are reduced (they do not have derivative suffixes). They are usually linked one to another by means of the suffix *-u-* (more rarely *-a-*) or, more generally, without intervening suffix. Only the last member has a grammatical marker. The homogeneous complex can be made of (a) several nouns: *parthenos-u-ŋiss-u-Marian* 'Saint Mary' (lit. 'virgin-holy-Maria'); (b) a noun with a pronoun or a numeral: *man-dippila* 'in this city' (lit. this-city-in), *dipp-u-wella* 'in one city' (city-one-in), or (c) several verbal formations: *ŋal-u-ulgren* 'seeing and listening' (lit. 'see-listening').

In the particular case that homogenous word clusters appear in enumerations, the connective function is fulfilled by the connective postposition *-de...-de-kel* 'and... and.' Case suffixes accumulate on the last member of the postposition, following the last element of the complex: *ŋešša-denal-de-on-tan-itt-u-jawė-de-kel-ka* (St., epilogue, 4) 'for Ṅešš of Atwa and his wife Jauê' (lit. 'Ṅešš of Atwa-and-his-wife-Jauê-too-ACC').

(2) Lack of homogeneity and loose integrity are distinctive features of the peripheral word cluster. It is formed by nouns and it has a logical (non-finite, participial) or grammatical (finite, verbal) predicate. Nouns in this word cluster are truncated.

Nominal suffixes accumulate at the end of the last member of the peripheral word cluster, i.e., at the predicate so that the word cluster appears as if it would be incorporated in the noun.

Peripheral word clusters with participial predicates usually play the role of dependent attributive clauses. The participial predicate agrees in number and case with the noun complex: *wiá-lo it-u-ko-ren-taratilo-kissela-pesildo* (C, 39) 'Woe to the man who talks in the course of the Eucharist in the church!' (lit. 'woe man-of-sacrament-in-partaking').

Attributive clauses adopt the form of peripheral word clusters with verbal (finite) predicates. All suffixes of the nouns in the attributive clause mechanically accumulate on the predicate: *ay-on-kumpu-tuskantelo-unnusin-ka-lo tan kissela utuddre* (M, 9) 'I will donate to his church the egg that it has first laid' (lit. 'I-and egg-in-the-beginning-(she-)gave.birth his to-church I.sacrifice').

(3) Nominalized word clusters are non-segmentable, and words in them are not truncated. Such word clusters, which are regular dependent clauses, form part of the main clause as its only constituent (be that as either a complement clause or an adverbial clause). They are formed with suffixes and postpositions as well as with one word to that effect. These markers are mechanically added to the last element of the complex, that is, to the predicate. The complement clause is formed like a nominalized word cluster, but with the accusative suffix: *ul-lo yera... koñilla-gille-jimittuphphisan-ka... gindatten-tratka-ayka-okkradissan-ka. wekke-gelinkittida-ayka-kitissan-ka* (St., 15) 'you know that they spit upon my face... and that they put on me a thorny crown, and that they dressed me in scarlet clothes' (lit. '(you) and knowing... to.face-they-spitted.upon-ACC... thorny-crown-me(-they)-putted-ACC... scarlet-clothes-me-dressed-ACC').

When the locative case marker and the postposition *-jun* 'from behind, because of' are attached to a nominalized word cluster, the result is a causal clause: *ŋapek' awėsi-lo-jun* (M, 44) 'because I have committed sin' (lit. 'sin-I-did-LOC because.of'). The nominalized owrd cluster then resembles an adverbial clause.

Specific temporal clauses, where there is some elaboration regarding the specifics of the time sequence (formal expression of continuativity, perfectivity, etc.), are sometimes formed like causal clauses (same locative case marker, but different postposition): *tijjaygul-de-ŋapekaėgul-de-kel-ka...pajesi-lo-kalo-yon* (St., 23) 'After I discuss the virtue and the sin' (lit. 'virtue-and-sin-too-and discuss-LOC-after').

Syntax of the simple clause

58 Word order. In ON, as in the majority of languages of the agglutinative type, a fixed SOV word order prevails: *man-ittil-lon... šaakka gall' isna* (M, 52) 'that woman... opened the door.'

The complement in genitive precedes the word it complements: *jelguna ilalte* 'execution of the times (lit. of-times-execution)'; *appogin mañil* 'skipper's eye'; *an tota* 'my son.'

Adverbials are distributed in between, but there is no fixed place for them. Word order only plays a grammatical role in the double accusative construction which will be described below.

Under certain circumstances, word order can be altered (needless to say, this is due to the influence of the Greek original). In general, information structure (the theme-rheme arrangement) is not modified by altering word order, but with the help of focal particles.

59 Case functions. The subject (nominal, pronominal, or participial) is marked with the nominative.

Those parts of the sentence that are not formally connected to any other part take the absolutive case. In first place, the subject of a denominative clause: *ŋokkora... ŋiss-u-minana* (M, prologue) 'The miracle... (of) Saint Mena.' In second place, nominal or participial predicates: *ur-u kosmosin pikita-ke* (Mth., XVII, 11) 'You, the light of the world' (lit. 'you world light(-is)').

(1) The absolutive case also functions as vocative: *papa-ŋissa* (Jn., XVII, 11) from Greek *páter hágie* 'Holy Father'; *papa-tijkatta* (ibid., 25) from Greek *páter díkaie* 'Right Father.'

Lastly, proper names take the absolutive before verbs meaning 'to name, call, mention': *tan taŋiska iēsusiá oke*, lit. 'his name Jesus naming,' from *kaí ekálesen tó ónoma autū iēsūn* 'And he uttered a name for him: Jesus' (Mth., I, 2); *tan taŋiska Emmanuela ókarrana* (ibid., 23) (lit. 'his name Emmanuel (they) will.call'), from *kaí kalésun tó ónoma autū Emmanuēi* 'And they will utter a name for him: Emmanuel.'

(2) Genitive is the case that marks the modifying noun.

(3) Accusative is the case that marks direct object: *tan wiñjika... ŋa-sin* (Mth., II, 2) (lit. 'his star... seeing-for'), from Greek *éidomen gár autū tón astéra* 'For we saw His star.'

We have mentioned that some verbs govern a double accusative. In the Lectionary, the Greek accusative of the direct object and the dative of the indirect object demanded by the verb 'to give' (*dídōmi tiní tí* 'to give something to someone') are both marked with accusative in ON: *pawuka takka tissin* (Jn., XVII, 2) (lit. 'authority him (you) gave'), from *édōkas autō eksusían* 'you gave Him the authority.' Moreover, the double accusative construction is attested with the verb *pilligir-* 'to reveal, disclose,' *kitir-, okkir-* 'to put on,' *pesatir-* 'to recount.' In these cases word order helps to distinguish one argument from the other: the direct object appears always first, and the "quasidirect" appears in second place: *tratka ayka okrá-dissan* (St., 15) 'they put on me the crown' (lit. 'crown me put.on'). Interestingly enough, all attested examples of double accusative follow causative verbs.

(4) In the remaining cases, the indirect object is expressed by the dative. The other cases are used to express various adverbial functions.

60 There are three types of predicates in ON: verbal, converbial, and nominal. In the first case a personal form of the verb carries out the function of predicate, in the second case, a coordinative converb and, in the third case, a noun in the absolutive with the focal particle or the linking verb *in-* 'to be.' Verbal and converbial predicates may appear in both voices, the nominal only in the intransitive active (expressing state). The following actualizing particles may appear after the nominal and participial predicates:

(1) *-lo* (the most often found ending): *istawrosil khristianosriguna teegta-lo* (St., 32) 'The Cross, the hope of Christians.'

(2) *-lē* marks predicates only for 1SG & 2SG referents, after a coordinative converb or when the predicate is a participle in the nominative: *ewartakarril-lē pissimme* (Phil., II, 17) 'even if I am being a sacrifice, I am glad (lit. 'donated I.be.happy-so'); *tekk-on onjara-lē* (Jn., XVII, 23) 'and you beloved them' (lit. 'them-and beloving').

(3) if the 2PL personal pronoun plays the subject role, the nominal and converbial predicate always take the particle *-ke*: *uru-kosmosin pikita-ke* (Mth., V, 14) 'You are the light of the world'; *koas-ke kosmoslá makitka magren-ende tulliŋana-so* (Jn., XVI, 33) 'In this life you shall have grief, but take courage!' (lit. having in.world grief, sorrowing-not be.in).

The particle *-ke* can appear also with nouns in absolutive plural: *ontakragué-ke* (M; L) 'Beloved! (PL).'

61 In ON there are one-member sentences too.

Denominative: *ŋokkora khristosin martyros-u-ŋiss-u-minana* (M, prologue) 'A miracle which Saint Mena, the Martyr of Christ (...).'

Impersonal: *awtakona* (St., 2) 'it came to pass';

If a personal pronoun plays the subject role, it is most frequently dropped out, so that the verbal predicate stands alone: *sal-u...-wekk-ende uruyó dekkigirmisse-lo* (St., 6) 'I shall not conceal from you any word' (lit. 'word-...-one-even from-you not-keep.in.secret').

62 In dependent clauses, the (verbal) predicate can appear in any of the three moods: indicative, imperative, and subjective. See section "Verb" about the indicative and imperative moods. If the dependent clause contains a verbal predicate, the subjective mood is expressed with the suffix *-imm* followed by the personal endings. In the case of nominal and converbial predicates, the subjective mood is expressed by the modal particle *-ma, -mē (-mi?), -m'*.

In independent clauses subjective mood is used:

(a) if the sentence includes direct speech (quoting the Gospels): *sennol iddimma dumokk-on gallatiddimme* (St., epilogue, 5) 'the one who asks shall receive, and to the one who knocks I shall be open for' (lit. 'asking he.receives to-knocking-and I.open'); *dola-m' orpa-ma* (C, 2) 'this bread, this wine.'

(b) in exclamative sentences and when expressing wishes: *kisselo pala-mē* (C, 5) 'Let him be excommunicated from the church!' (lit. 'from-church expelled-let').

If the verb *doll-* 'to want' appears in the main clause predicate and it has a complement clause, the main clause predicate takes the subjective mood too: *dollimme an-dute-gullo-min inguna-aydal-duddel-ka* (Jn., XVII, 24) 'I would like that they were in the place where I am' (lit. 'I.want-so me in-places these with.me be-ACC').

This phenomenon is also attested with the verbs *ei-* 'to know' and *pistew-* 'to believe': *ŋiden-ka taeimme* (Jn., XI, 24) 'I know that he shall rise again'; *pistewimme eir enen-ka* (ibid., 27) 'I believe that you exist' (lit. 'I.believe you existing'). Nothing else, apart from the accusative marker, highlights the syntactic link between the main clause and its dependent clause. Needless to say, the subjective mood marker in the main clause predicate is not intended to express modality in the main clause, but in the dependent clause, which is understood as a word cluster that functions as complement clause.

There are rarer cases when direct speech takes the subjective mood marker for subordinates *-a*. This phenomenon frequently occurs in the Pseudo-Chrysostom: *eikka ted immisse. en koērrō jookka kapatamē-à* (PC, XXI, 20–21) 'Did I not command you: do not eat of this tree?' (lit. 'to.you (I) commanded that-tree-of not-you.eat'). It is possible that here direct speech is understood as a certain subordinate variant of the purposive type (cf. 'in order to you not eat of that tree').

In the text mentioned above (the Pseudo-Chrysostom) we constantly find the subjective mood particle *-ma* used with the verb 'to call, to name,' i.e., as if it would be an indirect speech clause: *ŋaeià uk ōkijarre. tikanegué-ma sena. menen-non korosegué-ma* 'how I'll call you: "sheeps" or "sheperds"?' (PC, I, 7–9). Such a phenomenon is unheard of in other texts.

63 Information structure (theme–rheme arrangement). As already mentioned above, information structure is accomplished by marking rheme with the focal particle *-lo*. In this particular case, it seems that word order cannot be altered. The rheme may be any member of the sentence.

- Subject: *man-dippila-yon... kissel-lo nongara* (M, 39) 'and in that village was situated a church' (lit. 'this-in-city church-*lo* standing');
- Direct object: *in-kumpuka-lo man-kissela ken-dukarril-le* (M, 20) 'I will donate this egg to that church' (lit. 'that-egg-*lo* that-in-church I.donate');
- The nominal part of a compounded nominal predicate: *tan ŋogla duára miššangu-ketalle-yon miragué-lo issana* (M, 7) 'and all who lived in her house were also infertile' (lit. 'her in-home living-all-also-and infertile-*lo* were');
- Adverbial clause: *Philoxenitigille-lo jure* (M, 15) 'I am going to Philoxenite' (lit. 'Philoxenite-in-*lo* I.eat').

The rheme may be not just one word, but an entire word cluster: *áy-ón kumpu-tuskantelo-unnusin-ka-lo tan kissela utuddre* (M, 9) 'I will donate to his church the egg that it has first laid' (lit. 'I-and egg-in-beginning-(she-)gave.birth-*lo* his in-church I.donate').

Syntax of the compound sentence

64 A part of the dependent clauses that appear in the ON corpus is represented by peripheral and nominalized word clusters. Strictly speaking, the only dependent clauses that can be identified in the ON corpus are comparative, temporal, conditional, purposive, and indirect speech clauses. They can be formally divided into postpositional and modal.

Comparative and specific-temporal clauses are postpositional. The remaining dependent clauses (including here non-specific temporal ones) are modal.

(1) In <u>postpositional</u> dependent clauses, the link with the main clause is expressed by a postposition, connective, or case-governing. Unlike the nominalized word cluster, case-governing, and connective postpositions can be directly attached to the predicate.

Comparative clauses are marked with the postposition *-kello* 'like, similar to that': *kosmosla-gil ayk itrésin-kello. ay tekka kosmosla-gil itasse* (Jn., XVII, 18) 'As you sent me into the world, so I have sent them into the world' (lit. 'to.world me (you) sent-like I them to.world sent').

Specific temporal clauses are marked with the postposition *-kalo* 'after,' *-pawu* and *-pawuka* 'until, as long as,' *-tawklo* 'when': *kosmoska pešše-pajeri-pau* (St., 23) 'Until I will judge the world' (lit.

'world judge-I.shall-until'); *jimmilguna awtakeran-pawuka* (Mth., V, 18) 'until all is accomplished' (lit. 'of.all happens-until'); *ten ŋapeguk ostirajeri-tawklo-á* (Rom., XI, 27) 'when I take away their sins' (lit. 'their sins I.remove when').

(2) Non-specific temporal, conditional, purposive, and indirect speech clauses are <u>modal</u>. Thus they correspond to each other. The temporal link in compound sentences is expressed only by the sequence of verb tenses and the endings' short forms in the predicate clause:

- *kissel galliminin kipran* (C, 32) '(those who) eat when the church still is not open' (lit. 'church not-open they.eat'). Here we expect a concessive link, but formally we have a temporal link.
- *suáy-tuskon ukrigul ŋokajoruan-non dipp-u-weddo kisana* (M, 36) 'When the days of three months had gone by, they came to a town' (lit. 'of-months.three days they.passed-but in-town-one (they) came'). This is the only example of an anterior tense used in a dependent clause (remember that the anterior is only used in modal clauses).
- *kosmos-wattoka peššajeri-lo istawros-u-ŋokkol-lon an yonoyo-lo ŋonjanna* (St., 18) 'When I will have the entire world judged, on my right hand shall rest the Holy Cross' (lit. 'world-all judge-shall-I Cross-Holy me in right.hand rest-shall').

Main clauses and non-specific temporal clauses trigger the same sequence of verb tenses (temporal relationships) with respect to the conditional clause. Here the dependent clause predicate also takes the conditional marker -*ko*.

ále-sin ŋodil ayka mudwukon-no' philoxenitigille-lo jure (M, 15) 'Truly, if the Lord guide me, I am going to Philoxenite' (lit. 'truly-so lord me if-he.accompanies in-Philoxenite I.go'); *wel segega jora-kia-kappan-no manin ŋapeka... paskarre* (C, 49) 'If someone comes on an empty stomach and eat, I will punish his sin' (lit. 'one empty.stomach coming if-eat of-that sin... I.punish').

There is only one example of an irreal conditional, where the dependent clause predicate has the marker -*enkan*, while the main clause predicate appears in the indicative mood: *ŋoda eiri eñno duar-enkan an eŋŋal dimedra-lo* (Jn., XI, 21) 'Lord, if you had been here, my brother would have not died' (lit. 'lord you here be-if my brother not-die').

The semantics of the purposive clause include the notion of condition (in an inverted manner, the action of the main clause surfaces as the condition for the action of the dependent clause, and not the other way around as in the regular conditional clause) and subjectivization. In consequence, the purposive clause predicate contains a verbal formation in the conditional mood (without tense markers having the suffix -*ko* and a particle) together with the subjective particle for dependent clauses -*a*: 1SG: *tak'aygil tok'-arre-so kapkói-ó-á* (M, 34) 'Boil it and bring it to me so that I may eat it' (lit. 'him me boiling-bring him-in.order.to'); 3SG: *sortok' iskelisna tekka pistakkon-no-á* (ibid., 64) 'And she asked the priest to baptize her' (lit. 'to.priest (she) asked her baptize-in.order.to'); 1PL: ...*inin jurika irió-tjó ulgrá kosmosi-wattola jawatijjikou-ó-á* (St., 12) 'In order to us hear from you the reason of that and proclaim (it) to the entire world' (lit. 'of.that reason from.you hearing in-world-entire we.proclaim-in.order.to'); 2PL: *ininka udgille pesijeril. tokinnaweka aya konko-á-lo* (Jn., XVI, 33) 'This I told you, that you would have peace in me' (lit. 'this to.you I.say peace in-me you.have-in.order.to'); 3PL: *in taŋsloko tekka idñije-so. werinil dukoan-no-á* (ibid., XVII, 11) 'Keep them in your name... that they may be one' (lit. 'to.you name-after them preserve one they.are-in.order.to').

Lastly, when the action expressed in the indirect speech clause works independently of the action expressed in the main clause, the indirect speech clause shows an absolutive predicate (i.e., with the full form of the personal endings, this is a unique strategy dependent clauses), instead of the consecutive predicate found elsewhere. The predicate of the indirect speech clause takes only the subjectivizing modal particle -*a*: *anke-so eyudadal sola-dumatijjodo min awtakra-á* (C, 28) 'Remember what happened with Judas the traitor' (lit. 'remember with-Judas-traitor what it.was.done-(ABS)'); *tekka égidjisna isló khristosi unnutakona-á* (Mth., II, 4) '(He) inquired of them where the Christ was to be born' (lit. 'them (he) asked in-which Christ be.born-(ABS)').

(3) There is still one peculiar way to join complement and attributive clauses: relatives. In this case, the dependent clause subject is not in the nominative, but in the full (subjective) form of the genitive, and plays the attributive role of the word in the main clause that governs the dependent clause: *sala... iisusi-khristosina-lo... pesa-lo* (St., prologue) 'A speech which Jesus Christ (...) spoke' (lit. 'word Jesus-Christ... saying'); *awtakona ukrigulo wello en añjna saïtengun ŋaddildo ákin* (ibid., 2-3) 'It came to pass: when one day our Saviour was sitting on the Olive Mount (lit. happened in.days in.one to-our Savior of-Olives on-the-mount sits); see also the first sentence in the sample text (M, prologue).

TEXT

An Old Nubian Text
with Translation and Glossary

The Miracle of Saint Menas

[In 1994, G.M. Browne published his interpretation of this important ON text (note the unspoken convention that the form "Menas," from Greek *Mēnas*, is used in reference to the title, but "Mena," from Nubian ⲙⲏⲛⲁ, is reserved for the body of the text).

The best way to compare both Browne and Smagina's conceptions about the ON grammatical structure is to analyze their rendition of the text. Since the present work is a translation of Smagina's grammar, our English translation reflects the peculiarities of the original Russian, regardless of the differences which it may present with Browne's version. Only after Smagina's has been checked against Browne's, the comparison with a third party - Van Gerven Oei's translation (2012), see pp. 62-127 for glossed text - will become more profitable.

Note that Smagina's version included the facsimile of the first page, whereas Browne offered a facsimile of the entire work (pp. 91-108). As these are now easily accessible, we have not reproduced them here. Word segmentation in the transliteration below are Smagina's.]

Transliteration

0. ŋokkora khristosin martyros-u-ŋiss-u-minana awsa-lo. tillin tokinnawėlo amin.
1. ontakraguė-ke.
2. itt-u-wel-lo dipp-u-wella duára. álexandren šikgula.
3. tar-on mira ágen-de unnaramenna-lo. ŋak'-ende' ask'-ende.
4. iñitt-u-ŋuktlo. diyk-on koá-lo enona.
5. šewattkon konmenna-lo.
6. in-ŋeyn-juriá iá-yon tan' aylla maïkarisna.
7. tan ŋogla duára-miššangu-ketalle-yon miraguė-lo issana. medjunin-taygul. tuygul. dutrapi-gulo-kiyskillo.

8. ukrugulo well-yon. man'ittil khristïanosigun iliwgul pesran ulgra. toykaguė-sin-ŋiss-u-minana-mareótin-kissela-awjilguka. tariá pessna.
9. ále-sin ŋiss-u-minan tillil an dutrapigula wekka unne-s' ilenkonno. ȧy-on kumpu-tuskante-lo-unnusin-ka-lo tan kissela utuddre.
10. ukur'-diel' awtakon-non. dutrapigula wel juntuŋa kumpun kakilwekka unnusna.
11. man'ittil-lon kumpuk' en'ita ámando'sukka kisna. medjun-tal'-wel'dal. awik éla man-kumpuka ŋiss-u-minan kisse-maréotioŋonjilla-gil iteni-á.
12. awl'-philoxenitigil-jodra-meddaŋol'wekk'on éla. pessna ittil ágoppigille. pisse-so pap-o-ágoppa.
13. tar-on pessna. ik-ketal pisse-so.
14. ittil-lon pessna. ále-sin inno tukren isgil jodin.
15. apoggil pesara. ále-sin ŋodal áika mudwukon-no' philoxeniti-gillelo jure.
16. ittil-lon pessna. magren-non aydal untik' awá philoxenitigille ayik' eddal kojue-so.
17. ágoppil pesara. manno minka dollina-ï.
18. ittil pesara. ŋiss-u-minan kissegille-lo jure.
19. ápoggil-lon pessna. id-de ellino'inil-lē kissela mink awarrinna.
20. ittil pesara. in-kumpuka-lo man-kissela kenduk'arril-le. ŋiss-i-minan tillil itkin kojirka ayka denkon-no-á.
21. ále-sin unnre énen-non. khristiánosanádimme.
22. ápoggil pesara. itta. id-de aēttaka-ta-mē.
23. magirkon'-ende in-kumpuk-on ayka dine-so.
24. ay-sin penutuddre-sin.
25. ir-on in ŋooggille gipirte-so in ogjil ŋegimenkonno-á.
26. ittil-lon pistewá kumpuka tan' ila' utratirsna.
27. tar-on tan ŋooggille gipirtsna tan medjun-taaddal.
28. apoggil-lon kumpuka dum'-ita asin-tula kena kappa-sewéla uskursna. philoxenitió kien-pawka.
29. ukri-diygul ŋoka-joruan-non. philoxenitin gaaddo kisna.
30. ogjil-lon kumpuk' agora is-u-irkane-widilla-gille gipirtsna.
31. ukrigullo wello-yon. ápoggil man-kumpuka áwn'-ásin-tula kappa-sewéla piyn ŋalen. in'tan' uskra ágorisska. pessna tan ŋalgille.
32. é tota in-kumpul islo issna-ka.
33. tar-on pessna. papo ir-u inka ankiminna-ï. itt-u-wenna ekka denjiska. ŋiss-u-minan kissela tijjana-s-a.
34. papil-lon pessna totigille. é álelo. tak' aygil tok'-arre-so kapkoï-o-a.
35. tan ŋal-lon tokka takka kenotron. kap'itirsna.
36. suáy-tuskon ukrigul ŋoka-joruan-non. kipp-u-weddo kisana.
37. áwkk-on man-dippin gaddo kenóossna.
38. kyriaken ukur'inin-non. ápoggil dippiddo keda-kisna. korek' itni-á.

The Miracle of Saint Menas

39. man-dippila-yon parthenos-u-ŋiss-u-marian kissle-lo ŋonjara.
40. tariá-yon tora-kisna. korek' itni-á.
41. triságion kiesin-no-kono-yon. kipta-miššan-non kaskaseldo timmisana. ȧgiósin amanka paynu-á.
42. apoggin mañil-lon gallitakon ŋiss-u-minaka pillaallo ŋilsna. nurt-u-ŋuluka' doka-kin. takk-on tuzin šak arrinnagra.
43. tar-on ŋalen tillik-unnol marian igongille gudala kiá wuápessna.
44. irió-ma-lo tillik-unnara Maria ayka awlose. ŋapek'-awési-lo-jun.
45. ŋiss-u-mina-yon widillo ŋonja pessna tadgille.
46. minka iddal awarre élin ukurro.
47. ŋod-u-anni-lo-sin-ma-lo torrasi.
48. ŋissil-lon man ogijka dumma tak urildo jagŋon. kumpu-in tan'na kipsil. dumal dutrap' añaraŋa tanna-tawȯ-ketal sukka pala kutta ŋonja tuskono jawisna.
49. ŋiss-u-mina-yon murtiddo ȧkil dutrapka tan awir-wello dumma tak'enéta pessna.
50. indo guse. inka-lo isse.
51. ŋiss-u-mina-yon man-ittin ŋoglo jora-kiá. šaakka kimma' óókirsna.
52. man-ittil-lon midil ki' šaakka gallisna.
53. ŋissil-lon pessna tadgille.
54. itta in-ditrapka dum'eta in dutrapigulo pelire-so. ikka unnatikkoan-no-á.
55. ik-ketalle-yon é itta ŋak unnarrasi tan taŋiska minaá óke-so.
56. in medjunin-tayguk-ketal-kello unnadimmana. on in tuygul.
57. ir-on é itta pistitti ite-so in ŋapegun tokderragille.
58. inka pesa-toka-yon. dumak-kono ŋissil miwtakra ŋissna.
59. ittil-lon dutrapka duméta tan dutrapigulo peliron. dumak-kono-kello unnisana. medjunin-taygul. on tuygul.
60. tar-u-ittil-ketalle-yon juntuŋa' ŋan kakikka unnusna.
61. tan taŋisk-on okisna minaá. ŋissna tadgil pesesin-kello.
62. tan medjunin-tayguk-ketalle-yon juntuŋa'-kello unnusana. ŋakka aska.
63. man-ittil-lon tan kokkanen ukrigul kiriŋuan-ŋi ŋiss-u-mina-kisselo jora-kisna. mareótió.
64. kisse-ŋissla kien-non. sortok' iskelisna tekka pistakkon-no-á.
65. sortol-lon dummija. teddo silela. tad-de-tan-ogjil-de-tan-ŋad'-de-tan-medjunigul-de-kek-ka pistarisna papil-de-oŋ-ŋal-de-on-sewart-u-ŋissil-de-ke-n taŋslo-ko.
66. ikarigra-yon khristianosa kelkinnan inin duárisana. ten añen ukra-miššanno.
67. ŋiss-u-mina-kissena-yon degeri'inin duárisana. ten darpneka kisse-gille kaka-jojokil. ten dien-pawuka.

68. *jimmilgul-lon in ŋokkor-dawikka ŋal-u-ulgren. tillika ŋoktirsana. ȯn niss-u-minaka. tanna-sin ŋokil on toėkil. el'-ȯn tawka-miššanno jelguna ellengulo-kieskillo. ȧmin:*

Translation

The miracle of Saint Menas

0. A miracle which Saint Mena, the Martyr of Christ, performed. In God's love, Amen.
1. Beloved!
2. A woman lived in a village, in the region of Alexandria.
3. And she, being infertile, could give birth neither a son nor a daughter.
4. She had a lot of perishable wealth.
5. But she did not have a heir.
6. And because of this(, knowing that?) she was ashamed, in her heart.
7. And all who lived in her house were also infertile: the servant-girls, the cows and even the chickens.
8. And one day, she hears how Christian women (or: shepards) tell about the miracles which they performe in the church of Saint Mena in Mareotes, and she said to herself:
9. "Here it is, truly, if the God of Saint Mena made one of my chickens give birth, I will donate to his church the egg that it has first laid."
10. When many a day passed, one of the chickens became pregnant and gave birth offspring, i.e., one egg.
11. And that woman went down to the river with a servant-girl, in order to find a boat and take that egg to the church of Saint Mena located in Mareotes.
12. And finding a boat ready (or: loaded) to go to Philoxenite, the woman said to the skipper: "Greetings, father skipper."
13. And he said: "Greetings to you too."
14. And the woman said: "Truly, when everything is ready, where will you go?" (or: "Truly, when you depart from here, where will you go?").
15. The skipper said: "Truly, if the Lord guide me, I am going to Philoxenite."
16. And the woman said: "If you have mercy on me, do me a favor and take me with you to Philoxenite."
17. The skipper said: "What do you want there?"
18. The woman said: "I am going to the church of Saint Mena."

19. And the skipper said: "But a heathen like you, what will you do in the church?"
20. The woman said: "I will bring this egg to that church, in order that the God of Saint Mena may give me fertility (or: offspring)."
21. "Truly, if I give birth, I shall become Christian!"
22. The skipper said: "Woman, do not be anxious!"
23. "Do not be anxious, and give me that (or: your) egg."
24. "For I will take it away."
25. And you return to your house, so that your husband will not fear for you.
26. And the woman believed and placed the egg in his hand.
27. And she returned to her house, with her servant-girl.
28. And the skipper took the egg, placed it within the hold [of the boat] and set it among the rest of the provisions for the trip to Philoxenite.
29. When many a day passed, he came to the shore of Philoxenite.
30. But the man forgot about the egg and returned to the place from where he departed.
31. And one day, the skipper saw within the hold of the boat among the rest of the provisions that egg, this one which he had placed and forgotten, he said to his son:
32. "Oh boy, where does this egg come from?"
33. And he said: "Father, you remember, a woman gave it to us, in order to take it away to the church of Saint Mena."
34. And the father said to the son: "Oh, indeed. Cook it and bring it to me so that I may eat it."
35. And when his son cooked and placed it before him, he took it and ate it.
36. When the days of three months had gone by, they came to a village.
37. And (they) beached the boat at the shore of that village.
38. When the Sunday day begun, the skipper went up to the village to receive the sacrament.
39. And in that village was situated a church of Saint Mary.
40. And he entered it to receive the sacrament.
41. And after the Trisagion, all the people assembled at the baptistery, in order to cross themselves with the water of the holy one.
42. And when the eyes of the skipper were opened, he saw Saint Mena brigthly (or: clearly), riding a white horse and holding a hunting spear (or: targeting a spear in flames).
43. And when he saw (that), he, in fear, approached the image of Saint Mary and shouted:

44. "May it be your will, Saint Mary, save me, because I have committed sin."
45. And again Saint Mena revealed himself and said to him:
46. "What am I to do with you today?
47. It is because my Lord's will that I came."
48. And when the Saint took that man and kicked him in the head, the egg, this one which he ate, suddenly became a living chicken, and came out from under him, stood up and at once squawked.
49. And Saint Mena, sitting on the horse, grasped the chicken by its two wings, took it up and said:
50. "For this I came, this I gave birth." (?)
51. And Saint Mena went to the house of that woman, knocked on the door and called (for her):
52. And that woman came running and opened the door.
53. And the Saint said to her:
54. "Woman, take this chicken and place it among your chickens so that they may give birth for you.
55. And also you, oh woman, when you give birth to a son, call his name Mena.
56. Also your servant-girls will give birth, and so will your cows.
57. And you, oh woman, receive baptism for remission of your sins.
58. And having said that, the Saint at once disappeared (?).
59. And when the woman place the chicken among her chickens, they at one started giving birth, the servantgirls, and so did the cows.
60. And also she, (that) woman, became pregnant and gave birth offspring, i.e., a son.
61. And she called his name Mena, according as the Saint had said to her.
62. And also her servant-girls became pregnant and gave birth to sons and daughters.
63. And that woman, when the days of her sickness had passed, went to the church of Saint Mena in Mareotes.
64. And when she came into the holy church, she begged the priest to baptize her.
65. And the priest took them, prayed for them and baptized her, her husband, her son, and her servants in the name of the Father and the Son and the Holy Ghost.
66. And thus they became Christians, and so they remained all the days of their life.
67. And being servants of the church of Saint Mena, they made their offering to the church until their death.

68. And all who saw this great miracle or listened (about it), gave glory to God and Saint Mena, whose is the glory and the power, now and forever, unto the times of the ages. Amen.

Glossary

[In order to avoid redundancy, most of Smagina's "...suffix, ...marker" have been erased. All interrogation marks are Smagina's.]

-a_1	absolutive
-a_2	coordinative converb
-a_3	subjective (in dependent clauses)
aettak-	'be afraid, worry, tremble'
ag-	'to sit, be for a while, live'
ágiósin aman	'holy water' (Greek hágios 'holy, saint')
agopp(i)	'skipper'
agor-	'to forget
ak-	cf. ag-
ale	'reality, truth; indeed'
alelo	'indeed' (locative of the word 'reality')
-al	adverbial derivation suffix
aman	'water; the Nile'
an	'my' (from ay 'I')
-an	3PL personal ending (short form)
-ana_1	3PL personal ending (full form)
-ana_2	imperative PL
-ana-s-a	supine PL (subject-object, from *ana_2-so-a_3)
ank-	'to remember'
ann(i)	'my' (possessive ending with epenthesis, postpositional, from ay 'I')
añ-	'to live'
añaraŋ-	'to come to live'
añe	'life' (from añ- 'to live')
-ar_1	imperfective converb
-ar_2	future (-an after /n/)
arrinnagir-	'to shake' (acc. to Zyhlarz) 'to intend, aim' (acc. to Griffith)

as₁	'daughter'
as₂	'section of the ship' (in context, 'hold, bottom')
aw-	'to do'
aw(i)	'boat, ship'
awir-	'wing'
awlos-	'to save, rescue'
awtak-	'to happen, turn out' (PASS of aw- 'to do')
ay₁	'heart, soul' (usually ayl, with definite article)
ay₂	'I'
-d	future
-dal	comitative
darpne	'sacrifice, oblation'
dawi	'big, great'
-de	'and, but'
-de...-de-kel	'and... and...'
deger	'community'
den-	'to give me, us'
-de-on... -de-on	'and... and...'
di-	'to die'
die₁	'death' (from di-)
die₂	'much; multitude' (from diy)
dipp(i)	'city, town, village'
ditrap	cf. dutrap
diy	'many, numerous; much'
-do	superessive
dok-	'to sit on a horse, to ride'
doka-ki-	'to drive up'
doll-	'to want'
du-	'to be, exist, remain'
dumal	'suddenly'
dumak-kono	'at once' (from *dumal-kono)
dumït-	'to grasp'
dumm-	'to grasp, to shake'
dutrap	'hen'
ė	'eh!' (interjection)

-e₁	infinitive
-e₂	1SG personal ending (full form)
-e₃	imperative PL
-e-s-a	supine SG (S/O, from *-e₃-so-a₃)
ed	cf. er
el	'now'
ėl-	'to find'
ėlle	'time'
ellinosi	'heathen' (Greek héllēnos, Modern Greek éllinos)
en-	cf. in-
-en	subordinative converb (from *-el-n₂)
-ende	'without'
-ende... -ende	'either... or...'
-eni-ȧ, -ini-ȧ, -ni-ȧ	supine SG (from *-en-i₂-a₃)
enit-	'to raise' (from *en-it-)
er₁	'we'
er₂	cf. ir
ėt-	cf. it-
gaar, gar	'coast, side'
gaddo	superessive of ga(a)r (from *gar-do)
gall-	'to open'
gallitak	'to be opened' (passive of gall-)
gar	cf. gaar
-gil, -gille	dative
gipirt-	'to give back, return'
-gu	PL
-guė	variant of absolutive PL or nominative PL
gudal-	'to fear, to be afraid'
-ha	cf. -a₃
i	'hand'
-ï	interrogative
-i₁	1SG personal ending (short form)
-i₂	supine SG
-i₃	epenthesis
iȧ-	'to know'

-iá	cf. -la
id	cf. ir
igon	'image, icon' (Greek *eikṓn*)
ik	cf. ir
ikarigra	'so, thus; therefore'
il-	'to talk' (?)
iliwgul	'women' (or 'shepherds'?)
-imm	subjective
in	'this'
in	cf. *en-* 'to be'
iñitti	'perishable' (?)
-ió	cf. *-lo*
ir	'you'
irkane	'beginning; birth'
is-	'to give birth' (?)
is?	'who?'
isgil?	'in what direction, where?' (from *is?*)
iskel-	'to ask for'
islo?	'where?' (from *is?*)
iss-	past of the verb *in-* 'to be' (?) (from *in-s-)
it-	'to take, receive'
itki	'conception' (from *it-*)
itt	'woman'
-(i)	object PL
jagŋ-	'to step, trample (upon)'
jaw-	'to scream' (?)
jel	'time' ('age'?)
jimmil	'any, each'
jo-	cf. *ju-*
jojok-	'to bring continuously'
joraki-	'to come'
ju-	'to go, travel'
-jun	'because of, due to' (postposition + locative)
juntuŋ-	'to conceive, to became pregnant'
-juriá	'because of, due to' (postposition + genitive)

-k'	cf. -ka
-ka	accusative
kak	'foetus, fruit'
-kane	denominal derivative suffix
-kante	denominal derivative suffix
kap-	'to eat'
kapp(?), kappa(?)	'food'
kaskase	'aspersorium' (from kas- 'to drawn, scoop'?)
-ke	focal particle (only 2PL)
ked-	'to rise, get up'
ken-	'to carry, bring'
kenduk-	'to bring, to donate' (from ken-)
kent(i)r-	'to bring' (from ken-)
kenóos	'to bear, remove, pull out' (from *ken-oos-)
-kello	'like, similar to'
kelkinnan	(?)
-ketal, -ketalle	'too, also'
khristianosi	'Christian' (Greek khristianós)
khristianosaŋ-	'to become a Christian' (Greek khristianós)
ki-	'to come'
kimm-	'to knock'
kie	'coming, arrival' (from ki-)
kipt(i)	'people, folk'
-kiskillo, -kieskillo	'to, until' (postposition + locative)
kiriŋ-	'to go, pass (through)'
kisse	'church'
ko-	'to have'
-ko₁	conditional (in conditional and purposive clauses)
-ko₂	'for, to' (postposition + locative)
kokkane	'weakness'
kon-	cf. ko-
kojir	'fertility, offspring, conception' (?)
koju	'to take with oneself' (from ko-ju)
-kono	'after' (postposition + locative)

kore	'communion, Eucharist'
kumpu	'egg'
kyriake	'Sunday' (Greek *kyriakē*)
-(i)l	definite article or participle marker
-lo$_1$	locative
-lo$_2$	focal (in nominal and verbal predicates)
-lon	'and, but'
-le	extension of some suffixes and postpositions
-lē	focal
-m,' -ma, -mē	subjective (in dependent clauses)
mag-	'to suffer, miss, grieve'
magir	'grieve, pain, agitation, anxiety' (from *mag-*)
maïk-	'to be ashamed'
man	'that'
mañ	'eye'
martyrosi	'martyr' (Greek *mártyros*)
meddaŋ	'to get ready'
medjun	'servant, slave'
medjunin-taa, medjun-taa	'(female) servant, slave'
-men	verbal negation
-mi	cf. *-ma*
mid-	'to run'
min?	'what?'
mira	'infertile' (from **m-ir-*, cf. *irkane* 'birth')
miššan	'all, any'
miwtakra-ŋil-	'to disappear'
mudu- (mudw-?)	'to defend, protect, permit'
murt(i)	'horse'
-(i)n$_1$	genitive (short form)
-(i)n$_2$	2PL & 3PL personal ending (short form)
-na$_1$	genitive (full form)
-na$_2$	2PL & 3PL personal ending (full form)
-ni-ȧ	cf. *-eni-ȧ*
-no	cf. *-lo$_1$,-lo$_2$*

-non	cf. *-lon*
-nu-ȧ	supine PL
-o	anterior
-o	cf. *-u*
-ȯ	cf. *-lo*
og(i)j	'man, husband'
ȯk-	'to name, call'
on-	'to like'
-on	'and'
-on...-on	'and... and...'
ontak-	'to be loved' (from *on-*)
ȯȯk(i)r	'to call' (with object SG)
oos-, os-	'to take out'
pap	'father' (absolutive: *papa* or *papo*)
parthenosi	'virgin (about Saint Mary)' (Greek *parthénos*)
-pawuka, -pawka	'to, until, as long as' (postposition + genitive)
pay-	'to write'
pelir-	'to place, put, lay'
penutir-	'to carry, take'
pes-	'to speak'
pesatok-	'to speak, say'
pi-	'to be (in), lay'
pillaal	'brightness' (?) (from **pill-* 'light')
piss-	'to be glad'
pistar-	'to baptize'
pistew-	'to believe' (Greek *pistewō*)
pistitt(i)	'baptism'
-r1	imperfective
-(i)r2	object SG
-ro	cf. *-lo*
-s	past
-s'	cf. *-so*
sew(i)	'other'
sewart(i)	'spirit'
seratti	'heir, successor'

silel-	'to pray' (Coptic šlēl)
-so	imperative
sorto	'priest'
suåy	'month, beginning of the month' (Coptic sua, suay)
sukk-	'to exit'
ša	'spear'
šaa	'door'
šik	'circle, region'
taa, ta	'girl' (PL: taygu)
tad	cf. tar
-tak	passive
takka, tak	accusative of tar
tan	genitive of tar
tar	'he, she, it'
tawk(i)	'time'
-tawo	'under'
taŋis, taŋs	'name'
ted	cf. ted
tijj-	'to give' (from tir-j-)
till(i)	'god'
tillik-unnol	'Mother of God' (absolutive: tillik-unnara)
timm-	'to gather'
tir-	'to give'
-t(i)r	causative
tokderra	'redemption'
tokinnawė	'peace, mercy'
tokk-	'to boil'
tot	'son, child'
toraki-	'to come inside'
torra-	'to come'
toyk	'strength' (PL: toykagui)
triságion	'Thrice Holy prayer' (Greek triságion)
tukr-	'to get ready, depart, come out' (?)
-tula	inessive, 'inside' (+ genitive) (from *tu 'inner')

tuskante	'beginning'
tusko	'three'
tuskono	'at once'
tuygu	'cows' (SG is unattested)
-u₁	1PL & 2PL personal ending (short form)
-u₂	anterior 3PL
-u₃	coordinative marker in word clusters (with truncated elements)
uk(u)r	'day'
ulg(i)r	'to hear'
unn-, unnu-	'to give birth'
unnat(i)r-	'to force to give birth, make fertile'
unt(i)	'love, mercy'
ur	'head'
usk(u)r-	'to lay, put'
utrat(i)r	'to lay, put' (from *utur?)
utud-	'to donate' (from *utur?)
-uŋ	cf. -ŋ
wel, wer	'one, certain'
widillo	'again' (?)
wo	'two'
wu- (wuȧ-?)	'to scream, to cry out'
-yon	variant of *-lon*
ŋa	'son'
ŋal-, ŋil-	'to see'
ŋape	'sin' (Coptic *nabe*)
ŋeg-	'to fight, to bit'
ŋey	'thing, issue, topic'
-ŋ, -aŋ, -iŋ, -uŋ	inchoative
-ŋi	predicate particle (in temporal clauses)
ŋil-	cf. *ŋal-*
ŋis-s-	'to see' + past (from *ŋil-s-*)
ŋiss(u)	'holy'
ŋod	'Lord'
ŋok, ŋook	'fame, honor'

ŋok-	'to pass'
ŋokajor-	'to pass'
ŋokt(i)r-	'to honor, glorify, worship' (from *ŋok, ŋook*)
ŋonj-	'to stand'
ŋoog, ŋog	'house'
ɲukt(i)	'riches, wealth'
ɲulu	'white'
ŋokkor	'miracle'

References

[We kept reference numbers as in the original Russian publication. Gaps in the numeration correspond to references on Modern Nubian in the original (Smagina's Old Nubian text is the first of a two-part book, the second part being devoted to Modern Nubian). Within the Scholarly Literature section there is a division between non-Russian and Russian publications, as is customary in Russion scholarly works. These references which are located at the very end do not have reference numbers, because they have not been used by Smagina.]

Sources

[2] Barns, J. 1974. "A Text of the Benedicite in Greek and Old Nubian from Kasr el-Wizz." *Journal of Egyptian Archaeology* 60: pp. 206-11.
[3] Browne, G.M. 1980. "A New Text in Old Nubian." *Zeitschrift für Papyrologie und Epigraphik* 37: pp. 173-78.
[4] Browne, G.M. 1980. "New Texts in Old Nubian from Qasr Ibrim, I." *Sudan Texts Bulletin* 2: pp. 16-33.
[5] Browne, G.M. 1981. "An Old Nubian Version of Mark 11.6-11." *Zeitschrift für Papyrologie und Epigraphik* 44: pp. 155-66.
[6] Browne, G.M. 1981. "An Old Nubian Fragment of Revelation." *Studia papyrologica* 20(2): pp. 73-82.
[7] Browne, G.M. 1982. "A Fragment of Ps.-Chrysostom from Qasr Ibrim." *Sudan Texts Bulletin* 4: pp. 1-10.
[9] Budge, E.A.W. 1909. *Texts Relating to Saint Mêna of Egypt and Canons of Nicaea in a Nubian Dialect, with Facsimile*. London.
[10] = [28]
[11] = [29]
[14] Plumley, J.M. 1980. "A Medieval Nubian Literary Texts." *Sudan Texts Bulletin* 2: pp. 34-41.
[16] Schäfer, H., and K. Schmidt. 1906. "Die ersten Bruchstücke christlicher Literatur in altnubischer Sprache." *Sitzungsberichte der Königlich Preussischen Akademie der Wissenschaften, Philosophisch-historische Klasse* 43(2): pp. 774-85.

[17] Schäfer, H., and K. Schmidt. 1907. "Die altnubischen christlichen Handschriften der Königlichen Bibliothek zu Berlin." *Sitzungsberichte der Königlich Preussischen Akademie der Wissenschaften, Philosophisch-historische Klasse* 44(1): 602-13.
[19] = [62]
[20] = [63]

Scholarly literature

[5] Ольдерогге, Д.А. 1929. "О некоторых египто-нубийских словах." *Сборник Египтологического кружка при Ленинградском государственном университете* 1: pp. 13-14.
[7] Розов, А.В. 1890. *Христианская Нубия. Историко-критическое и церковно-археологическое исследование*, ч. 1. Киев.
[8] Смагина, Е.Б. 1985. "Греческие заимствования в коптском и древненубийском языках." *Мероэ* 3: pp. 203-7.
[9] Смагина, Е.Б. 1979. "Древненубийский язык: письмо и фонология." *Вестник древней истории* 4: pp. 100-106.
[10] Смагина, Е.Б. 1979. "Формообразующие категории имени древненубийского языка." *VIII Всесоюзная конференция по Древнему Востоку, посвященная памяти академика В.В. Струве (2.II.1889-15.IX.1965). Тезисы докладов. Москва.*
[11] Смагина, Е.Б. 1980. *Язык древненубийских текстов*. Автореф. канд. дис. Москва.
[12] Смагина, Е.Б. 1983. "Опыт реконструкции одного древненубийского текста." *Вестник древней истории* 2: pp. 106-11.
[13] Тураев, Б.А. 1914. "Открытие нубийской христианской литературы." *Христианский Восток* 3(1): pp. 92-94.

[16] Adams, W.Y. 1977. *Nubia: Corridor to Africa*. Princeton.
[21a] Browne, G.M. 1979. "Notes on Old Nubian, I-III." *Bulletin of the American Society of Papyrologists* 16: pp. 249-56.
[21b] Browne, G.M. 1980. "Notes on Old Nubian, IV-V." *Bulletin of the American Society of Papyrologists* 17: pp. 37-43.
[21c] Browne, G.M. 1980. "Notes on Old Nubian, VI-VII." *Bulletin of the American Society of Papyrologists* 17: pp. 129-41.
[21d] Browne, G.M. 1981. "Notes on Old Nubian, VIII-X." *Bulletin of the American Society of Papyrologists* 18: pp. 55-67.
[22] Browne, G.M. 1981. "Arabic 'innamâ: An Old Nubian Analogue." *Göttinger Miszellen* 45: pp. 9-14.
[23] Browne, G.M. 1982. *Griffith's Old Nubian Lectionary*. Rome & Barcelona.

References

[24] Browne, G.M. 1982. "The Old Nubian Verbal System." *Bulletin of the American Society of Papyrologists* 19: pp. 9-38.

[27] Greenberg, J.H. 1962. *The Languages of Africa*. Bloomington (originally published in 1963 in *International Journal of American Lingusitics* 29[1-2]).

[28] Griffith, F.Ll. 1913. *The Nubian Texts on the Christian Period*. Berlin.

[29] Griffith, F.Ll. 1928. "Christian Documents from Nubia." *Proceedings of the British Academy of Sciences* 14: pp. 117-46.

[33a] Hintze, F. 1971. "Beobachtungen zur altnubischen Grammatik, I-II." *Wissenschftliche Zeitschrift der Humboldt-Universtät zu Berlin. Gesellschafts- und Sprachwissenschaflitche Reihe* 20(3): pp. 287-93.

[33b] Hintze, F. 1975. "Beobachtungen zur altnubischen Grammatik, III." *Altorientalische Forschungen* 2: pp. 11-23.

[33c] Hintze, F. 1975. "Beobachtungen zur altnubischen Grammatik, IV." *Nubia. Récentes recherches. Actes du Collague Nubiologique International au Musée National de Varsovie, 19-22 juin 1972*. Warszawa: pp. 65-69.

[33d] Hintze, F. 1977. "Beobachtungen zur altnubischen Grammatik, V." *Altorientalische Forschungen* 5: pp. 37-43.

[50] Michalowski, K. 1974. *Faras*. Warsaw.

[55] Reinisch, L. 1911. *Die sprachliche Stellung des Nuba*. Vienna.

[57] Stricker, B.H. 1940. "A Study in Medieval Nubian." *Bulletin of the School of Oriental Studies* 10(2): pp. 439-54.

[58] Tucker, A.N., and M.A. Bryan. 1956. *The Non-Bantu Languages of North-Eastern Africa*. Oxford.

[61] Zyhlarz, E. 1928. *Grundzüge der nubischen Grammatik im christlichen Frühmittelalter (Altnubisch)*. Leipzig.

[62] Zyhlarz, E. 1928. *Zur Stellung des Darfur-Nubischen*. Vienna.

[63] Zyhlarz, E. 1932. "Neue Sprachdenkmäler der Altnubischen." *Studies, Presented to F.Ll. Griffith*. Oxford: pp. 187-95.

[Browne, G.M. 1989. *Introduction to Old Nubian*. Berlin.]

[Browne, G.M. 1991. "Old Nubian Studies: Past, Present and Future." In W.V. Davies (ed.), *Egypt and Africa: Nubia from Prehistory to Islam*. London: pp. 286-93.]

[Browne, G.M. 1994. *The Old Nubian Miracle of Saint Menas*. Wien-Mödling.]

[Browne, G.M. 2002. *Old Nubian Grammar*. Munich.]

[Smagina = Смагина, Е.Б. 1986. *Древненубийский язык*. — Завадовский, Ю.Н., & Е.Б. Смагина, *Нубийский язык*. Москва: pp. 13-39 (grammar), pp. 71-80 (sample text).]

[Jakobi, A., and T. Kümmerle. 1993. *The Nubian Languages. An Annotated Bibliography.* Köln.]

[Van Gerven Oei 2012 = *The Miracle of Saint Mina.* ~ ⲅⲓⲥ ⲙⲓⲛⲁⲛ ⲛⲟⲕⲕⲟⲣ. Translated to Dongolawi (Andaandi) by El-Shafie El Guzuuli, translated to English by Vincent W.J. van Gerven Oei. The Hague/Tirana.]

www.ingramcontent.com/pod-product-compliance
Lightning Source LLC
Chambersburg PA
CBHW051133160426
43195CB00014B/2460